Code Equity:
Keying Girls Into Coding

Tara Linney

© 2018 Tara Linney
All rights reserved.

ISBN: **0692077707**
ISBN-13: **978-0692077702**

Preface	**5**
Part 1: Understanding Gender Inequity	**7**
Chapter 1: History of the Gender Gap	9
Chapter 2: Gender Bias in Education	23
Part 2: Keys for Gender Equity in Coding	**39**
Chapter 3: Get Frustrated	41
Chapter 4: Adopt the Iteration Mind-Set	51
Chapter 5: Ask Three before Me	61
Chapter 6: Utilize Pair Programming	71
Chapter 7: Allow the Student to Become the Expert	79
Chapter 8: Obtain Base Level Knowledge	87
Chapter 9: Reflecting and Learning Keywords	95
Part 3: Initiatives for Empowering Girls	**107**
Chapter 10: From Blogging Club to Coding Club	109
Chapter 11: Made with Code	117
Chapter 12: The Hour of Code—A Family Night	121
Chapter 13: Evolution from Co-ed to Girls Coding Club	125
Chapter 14: Technovation Challenge	129
Part 4: Linking Coding into the Curriculum	**137**
Chapter 15: Coding Progressions	139
Chapter 16: Integration in Math	143
Chapter 17: Integration in RLA, Writing and Language	161
Chapter 18: Coding Resources	177
Acknowledgements	**187**
Bibliography	**189**

Preface

Twenty-four boys and one girl. This was the makeup of the Coding Club that pushed me to focus in on and reassess how we as educators might create a more gender-equitable learning environment.

This book is written for the hundreds of thousands of educators in the world who have been stumped by the inequity that exists between boys and girls in our classrooms. Although this book is about creating gender equity in the teaching of coding, you will find that the practices that live within these chapters can be used across a variety of content areas.

The inequity in the world of technology as a whole has changed massively since the 1980s. When computing became "a thing," women were at the helm. Nowadays, women are being harassed, bullied, and unheard simply because they have an extra X chromosome.

As a society, we can work to create a more balanced opportunity for employment in the many technology-infused career fields that currently exist—as well as in the ones that don't exist just yet. However, before we begin to make changes to the outside, we must examine what is occurring on the inside. Through the identification of our own biases, we can begin to understand the impact that our choices in the classroom have on the students left in our care.

Within the contents of this book, we focus on equity, which is different from equality. *Equality* is ensuring that everyone has the same exact thing, quantity and all. *Equity* is the quality of being fair and giving each individual what he

Figure 1.0: Interaction Institute for Social Change | Artist: Angus Maguire

or she needs. When we talk about gender equity in coding, our focus is on creating equitable learning environments so that our students can thrive.

When I first set out to write this book, a member of my professional learning network, asked me, "What about the boys?" This question has come up a lot over the years and is one of the reasons for the title and topic of this book. Coding was originally a girls' field. Later, the boys came along and declared it was theirs. Now there is a focus centered on getting girls to code, as though no girl has ever coded before. The purpose of this book is to create opportunities for educators to build a gender-equitable learning environment for their students. Although the strategies focus on how to work toward building up girls' confidence in this field, the driving force behind it is to give girls what they need—to make their opportunities to understand coding more equitable.

This book is divided into four parts.

Part 1 focuses on the identification and understanding of gender equity—the historical context and basis as well as its debilitating features within the current technology industry.

Part 2 focuses on best practices for achieving gender equity. These best practices relate specifically to strategies for creating gender-equitable opportunities in the learning environment when teaching coding, with teaching approaches that are transferable to other content areas.

Part 3 focuses on highlighting learning opportunities, specifically geared toward empowering girls to learn how to code.

Part 4 focuses on the variety of ways in which coding opportunities can be integrated into a variety of reading, writing, arithmetic, and world-language content areas.

Part 1

Understanding Gender Inequity

In this section, we'll examine how the media has an impact on our students' confidence, ideas, and perceptions of their own abilities, and we'll find ways to mitigate these in the educational setting.

History of the Gender Gap

Starting with the Why

It is important to understand what the gender gap is and where it exists. As educators, when we're teaching our students, we often encounter a version of the example the media sets for them. Here we'll look at the importance of understanding the impact of gender equity on our society while examining the ways in which the different media groups are making strides to support or regress a more gender-equitable world.

History of Coding

The first computer programmer dates back to 1843, when mathematician Ada Lovelace (a woman) created an algorithm to calculate a sequence of Bernoulli numbers.[1] As a young girl, Ada was smitten with math and language. Transferring these content areas into publishing the first-ever computer program created a world of possibility for other young girls to follow suit in their coding endeavors. (It's important to note that there was a massive time difference between advances in the coding field due to focused attention on World War I [1914–1918].)

Almost one hundred years after the first coding advancement, we saw new efforts centered on a society developed during World War II (1939–1945). In 1938, Konrad Zuse (a man) built the Z1—the world's first binary digital computer—and the language to operate it. Later in 1941, he built the first fully functional program-controlled electromechanical digital computer, the Z3.

Then, in 1946, a team of six women formed to program the first fully electronic programmable computer with the Electronic Numerical Integrator and Computer (ENIAC) project. This was the very first computer of its kind and was used by the US Army as a post–World War II project.[2]

In 1952, mathematician Grace Hopper (a woman) completed the program A-0, which allowed the computing person to use English-like words instead of numbers to give the computer instructions. Much of the script-based coding that is used today can be attributed to her. From the advent of this new script-based process for coding, new languages began to emerge. The coding language FORTRAN was developed in 1957 by John Backus (a man) and an IBM team. COBOL (Common Business-Oriented Language) was created by a team of programmers in conjunction with the Pentagon in 1960.

In 2016, the *Hidden Figures*[3] movie was released about a group of African American mathematician women who worked for NASA (originally known as NACA: National Advisory Committee for Aeronautics) from the 1950s to the 1980s as some of the first-known "computers." Their job was to "compute" the calculations that would enable NASA to safely launch and land its space shuttles. With their knowledge, dedication, and support, NASA was able to have its first astronaut walk on the moon on July 20, 1969. These women—Katherine Johnson, Dorothy Vaughan, and Mary Jackson—had gone unnamed as "hidden figures" for nearly fifty years before writer Margot Lee Shetterly uncovered the true history of the country's first successful mission to the moon.

The coding language BASIC (Beginner's All-Purpose Symbolic Instruction Code) was developed by John G. Kemeny (a man) and Thomas E. Kurtz (a man) of Dartmouth College in 1964. Then, in 1967, Seymour Papert (a man) developed the LOGO coding language, which allowed students to type instructions as the turtle followed them, step by step, drawing each instruction on the screen. It wasn't until this particular coding language was invented that we began to consider the potential of students learning how to write code.

Pascal coding language was created in 1970 by Blaise Pascal (a man), which was applicable to both scientific and commercial applications. Dennis Ritchie (a man) and his team developed C coding language in 1972. C language has inspired many of the languages that are used in coding today.

When we look at some of these major developments in the coding industry from its inception to the 1970s, we can see that both men and women have been behind some of the industry's most notable advancements. There was a general concept of overall equity in the industry. This is important to note as we now begin to look at what has caused such a major dysfunction in society around women's entry into the field of computer science.

What comes next is not meant to seem as though women didn't experience inequity before 1984, but rather to highlight the impact that societal perspectives have had on women pursuing the field, especially in regards to the media's influence.

1984 was the year that video games became a huge hit. The first major game consoles were developed over the course of two decades: Atari (1977), Nintendo (1983), Game Boy (1989), Super Nintendo (1990), PlayStation (1995), and Nintendo 64 (1996). Marketing was geared toward boys, showing the boy as the hero or fighter in the games and the girl as an attractive damsel in distress or a prize to be won. As a young girl, when you see these examples on screen, it has an influence on what you choose to be. It's hard to dream or imagine when you can't see an applicable example of what you want to be. Just take a look at the titles in the following list to better understand how advertising worked to sell these games to boys.

The top ten video games of 1984 were the following:[4]

1. *The Last Starfighter*
2. *Gremlins*
3. *The Hitchhiker's Guide to the Galaxy*
4. *Break Dance*
5. *Dragon Slayer*
6. *Paperboy*
7. *Kung-Fu Master*
8. *Deus ex Machina*
9. *Duck Hunt*
10. *King's Quest: Quest for the Crown*

Paperboy focuses on a paper "boy." The *King's Quest: Quest for the Crown* focuses on his journey to the crown. As you can see from this top-ten list, the vast majority focused on the male gender as the heroes and protagonists within these games.

The media-driven gender stereotypes didn't stop there. In 1984, the top ten movies included an all-male lead cast of *Ghostbusters*, an overly sexual female cop amid a group of males in *Police Academy*, and a woman as an archaeologist's prize in *Indiana Jones and the Temple of Doom*. When we watch movies, we tend to view ourselves as one of the characters. If the only character matching our gender is the one who is always needing to be "saved," then we can begin to understand how girls might be developing a "help-me" complex geared toward outward perfection, with not much going on upstairs.

The top ten movies of 1984 include the following:[5]

1. *Beverly Hills Cop*
2. *Ghostbusters*
3. *Indiana Jones and the Temple of Doom*
4. *Gremlins*
5. *The Karate Kid*
6. *Police Academy*
7. *Footloose*
8. *Romancing the Stone*
9. *Star Trek III: The Search for Spock*
10. *Splash*

When *Ghostbusters* was remade in 2016, it was considered a box-office flop. The remake included a cast of comedic women to replace the men of the 1984 version, and its failure was attributed to a backlash against this gendered change.

Considering how these media examples infiltrated the homes of young boys and girls throughout society, it's easy to see why so few women have been entering technology-rich career fields since the 1980s. Compound that with the way in which women are treated for even considering a career in the male-dominated field, including reports of bullying and harassment in the notorious Silicon Valley, it's no wonder there has been such a shortage of and inequity for women entering (and staying in) the field of coding.

"Computers are for boys…What gets created in technology depends on who is doing the creating," said Marie Klawe of Harvey Mudd College in an interview with *PBS NewsHour*.[6]

On October 21, 2014, NPR's *Morning Edition* recorded a segment titled "When Women Stopped Coding."[7] This segment highlighted how the number of women joining the ranks of computer programmers had increased over time, but when the year 1984 hit, the number "flattened and then plunged." In the interview, Patty Ordonez talks about her experience with getting into coding in college. Coming from a strong high-school math background, she had confidence in her ability to learn how to code, which was quickly deflated when she witnessed the perceived confidence of her male counterpart. After struggling in the course, Ordonez was able to earn a C, *her first C ever*! She ended up dropping out of the program altogether. And that perceived confidence of her male counterpart was due to the fact that he had a home computer.

There are two glaring problems that emerge from this 1984 example. One is the issue of access, and the other pertains to gender confidence.

For the remainder of this chapter, we'll address the issue of gender stereotypes in marketing and how it links to an issue of equity in the world of girls and their potential career choices, including computer science. In chapter 2, we'll look at how education mimics media and the ways in which educators can help to mitigate the inequities that girls face in the technical fields.

Gender Stereotypes in Marketing and Media: The Good, the Bad, and the Ugly

Many good things have come from the media in the last decade in an effort to get more girls interested in coding. In 2014, Linda Liukas launched a Kickstarter campaign to write a book titled *Hello Ruby* as a literary way of inspiring young girls to learn how to code.[8] The funding period for the Kickstarter was from January 23, 2014, to February 22, 2014. In that time, Liukas was able to

Figure 1.1: Hello Ruby book

raise $380,747 from a $10,000 goal with the help of a total of 9,258 backers. This book offers a beautiful entry into inspiring girls' interest in coding through the use of a relatable story that highlights the challenges of life and coding. With the introduction of coding language nomenclature, *Hello Ruby* gives girls a head start in understanding the meaning of computing terms while also providing an activity book for some unplugged coding activities. The exercises in the back of the book get the girls up on their feet, walking them through the steps of everything from sequencing to debugging to creating unplugged programs.

In April 2016, another Kickstarter project titled *Goodnight Stories for Rebel Girls: 100 Tales to Dream Big* was started by Elena Favilli and Francesca Cavallo.[9] The goal of this book was to give girls a variety of stories on real-life women throughout time who have shattered barriers of gender stereotypes. With a funding period from April 27, 2016, to May 26, 2016, the writers were able to raise a total of $675,614 from a $40,000 goal with the support of 13,454 backers. The mere success in the funding of these books

Figure 1.2: Goodnight Stories for Rebel Girls

shows that there is a major desire throughout the book market for girls to live their dreams, regardless of the voices in society that tell them to stay in their gender-specific lanes.

Barbie decided to jump on the coding bandwagon to help promote girls in coding in 2010. It started with the movie *Barbie: I Can Be a Computer Engineer*, which was later turned into a book and published in 2013.[10] In the book, Barbie decides to make a computer game. Notably, she is *only* designing the game and getting the boys to do the coding to actually make the game function. When her computer gets a virus and she accidentally transfers the virus to her sister's computer, Barbie asks a female teacher for help. The teacher tells her how to get rid of the virus, so what does Barbie do? She takes that information and gets two boys to fix it for her, saying that it will save time if they fix it rather than trying to fix it herself. In the story, Barbie took the credit for creating a computer game *and* for fixing her sister's computer when all she actually did was take a shortcut and get the boys to do the work for her, further perpetuating the stereotype of girls having to rely on boys to do the heavy lifting.

One day in 2014, blogger and mother Pamela Ribon noticed the book at a friend's house. At first excited by the cover title and the free stickers, she proceeded to read the book and discovered the true message that had been disseminated to Barbie-loving girls throughout the world for *four years prior* (via the *Barbie: I Can Be a Computer Engineer movie*). She was so taken aback that she wrote a blog post (the title of which pretty much sums it up) that went viral in November 2014.[11]

Mattel received so much backlash from the reviews of this newly rediscovered book that they pulled it from stores and online retailers. If you're lucky, you might be able to find this hypocritical gem at a used bookstore or yard sale.

In 2016, after much help from actual women in coding, Barbie underwent a makeover, creating a more palatable version of Barbie Programmer. This version of the doll, Barbie Careers Game Developer sets the stage for how girls could be approaching computing jobs. In 2017, Barbie went on to partner with Tynker to create a *PetVet* programming experience that engages girls with coding in a veterinarian office community.[12]

Contrast the *Hello Ruby* and *Goodnight Stories for Rebel Girls* examples with the *Barbie: I Can Be a Computer Engineer* book, and we can see what stereotypes emerge. On the one hand, we have two books that promote an inspirational curiosity mind-set, and on the other, we have a book that promotes the stereotype of defaulting to asking a boy for help when we hit a roadblock. In part 2 of this book, we'll look at instructional practices you can incorporate to empower girls to look inside to find their own confidence while developing an iteration mind-set rather than defaulting to quitting or getting someone else to debug their programs.

Some websites have offered another way of respecting girls as they promote a culture of building girls' confidence in coding from a young age. Releasing its employment report in 2014, Google took a deep look at its diversity and decided to create opportunities for young people to help close the gender gap in employment over time. In the summer of 2014, Google launched the positive website MadewithCode.com, which teaches girls how to code by connecting directly with a variety of their creative interests. This site offers a series of mentor videos showcasing actual women in their careers using coding. These two-minute videos offer a snapshot of the creative career possibilities that integrate coding with another field of interest, such as dance, music, art, science, or medicine, to name a few. In addition, the site offers a variety of coding activities for girls to work on, which allows them to foster creativity, critical thinking, and communication skills while harnessing their computational thinking skills.

In December 2014, Flocabulary released a video titled *Top 10 Reasons to Code* to inspire children and educators to see the benefits of learning how to code. Although the video visually featured far more men than women reaping the benefits of learning how to code, they did bring up a few good verbal points to highlight the need for more women in the coding industry. First, after reason number nine, the narrator says, "*Not too many women in the code game, but now I think it's time for that to all change,*" addressing the fact that women are underrepresented in the coding world while also expressing a strongly held opinion that it's "*time for that to all change.*" He later raps about changing the world and how coding could be used in "*medical research to help cure cancer.*" Later in the book, we'll talk more about the ways to pique girls' interests in coding. This video does a good job of recognizing multiple reasons or drives for learning how to code, including speaking to the "helper" and "fixer" mentality of girls.

Then there's the gender-stereotyping outcry of 2017. Unfortunately, this incident took place at the same time as the Technovation Challenge, a challenge where groups of girls from around the world come together to find a problem in their community and code an app to address the solution.[13] A Google employee, James Damore, wrote a manifesto titled "Google's Ideological Echo Chamber" and posted it on the company's message board. He was subsequently fired after the media got ahold of it. In it, Damore highlights some of the same points made in the 2013 Barbie book, stating that *"representative viewpoints are important for those designing and testing our products, but the benefits are less clear for those more removed from UX (user experience design)."*[14] By painting the picture of what a girl is compared to what a boy is and providing gender differences for ambition as a reason for why so few women enter coding career fields, Damore's perspective created a viral conversation around women in tech careers. Google does not support this ex-employee's viewpoint, but the backlash is something that is highly likely to cause similar conversations to arise across the industry in the coming years.

The advertising industry has also made some major errors in the last decade when it comes to gender equity in coding. Although the United States has created its own host of battles on gender stereotyping, Britain has taken the most dramatic, sweeping action within an industry. In July 2017, Britain began cracking down on gender stereotypes in the advertising industry. In December 2016, one company created a commercial for baby formula showing a baby girl growing up to be a ballerina and a baby boy growing up to be a mathematician. A series of other British ads have essentially stereotyped women, as many US ads have for a long time. The difference here is that Britain is actually doing something about it. In 2016, the Advertising Standards Authority (ASA) of Great Britain opened an inquiry into gender stereotyping in ads to determine whether the advertising codes and the ASA's enforcement of them were being upheld. The inquiry found six categories of gender stereotypes: roles, sexualization, body image, objectification, characteristics, and mocking those who do not conform to stereotypes.[15] As a result of this study, Britain is in the midst of creating new advertising regulations and will be instituting these new bans in 2018, making it illegal for advertisers to promote gender stereotyping in their ads.[16]

It will be interesting to see what the US Federal Trade Commission does to better regulate the gender stereotyping that exists in US-made advertisements. This full ban in Britain comes during a time when American women are facing the stripping away of their rights in a presidency that objectifies women as a kind of rite of passage.

Gender Gap

A gender gap is a discrepancy in opportunities, status, pay, and attitudes between men and women.[17] Equity is fair access to what an individual needs in order to be successful. Equality is being provided with equal status, rights, opportunities, and/or pay. Throughout the history of occupations, there exists both a gender gap and either gender inequity or gender inequality.

Since the 1890s, there have been gender gaps in occupations throughout the United States.[18] In 1890, 15 percent of women between the ages of twenty-five to forty-four reported having an outside-of-home occupation compared to 60 percent of men of the same age range who were gainfully employed outside the home.[19] By 1940, the percentage of women in this age range went up to 30 percent. By 1970, it went up to 47 percent, increasing to 76 percent by the year 2000.

With the narrowing of the overall gender gap in occupations, the gender gap in pay in the working world has also experienced a narrowing since 1980. In 1980, women were paid 60 percent of what men made. Compare that percentage to the 1994 figure, where women earned 74 percent of what men did.[20] In 2015, women were paid 83 percent of what their male counterparts received.[21]

Although as a society we are continuing to move forward in closing the gender pay gap, there is still much work that needs to be done in closing the gender gap in the computer-science occupations.

In 1984, women made up 37 percent of the computer-science majors. By 2014, that number had dropped to 18 percent.[22] If this percentage continues to drop, or even stagnate, then we'll begin seeing an economy where men are the sole decision makers. Men will continue to be the ones with the highest-paying jobs in the computing field, earning wages that are 28 percent higher than that of women performing the same job function.[23] Computing jobs are the number-one source of new wages in the United States, and they are expected to grow at twice the rate of all other jobs. However, if women continue to leave the field, those new wages will continue to go straight into the pockets of men, dredging up images of the man being the sole income earner in all settings, making all the decisions within a household, career fields, and within society.

Studies show that women who try advanced-placement computer science in high school are ten times more likely to take a computer-science course in college.[24] In 2007, a mere 2,665 female students took the advanced-placement computer-science exam, representing only 18 percent of the total number of test takers.[25] In 2017, this number skyrocketed to over twenty-nine thousand girls, representing approximately 27 percent of the total number of test takers. This is an *enormous* gain. Although this is an amazing advancement, we still need to do more work in growing both the percentage and the number of girls who take on computer science. When we compare these percentages to the hiring practices of tech companies, we can see the transference of underrepresentation from childhood into adulthood.

In chapter 2, we'll examine gender bias in education so that we can begin to recognize the biases that exist within our learning communities. We'll look at gender biases that take place in education as well as strategies to eliminate those biases. The remainder of the book will introduce ways to dispel these myths of gender stereotypes so that we can see the whole child and be able to advocate for the empowerment of a gender that has been underrepresented in a male-dominated community for far too long.

Gender Bias in Education

When addressing the gender stereotypes that exist in education, it's important to first distinguish between the origins of these mind-sets and to understand that they could have originated from any one of three different places: the family, the larger community, or the media. This is precisely why knowing our students and their backgrounds is incredibly important when we're discussing the equitable learning opportunities for an entire gender. Sometimes cultures hold girls back, and culture is a hard thing to change; thus, we need to understand which aspect of a student's life is prohibiting her advancement and progress in a field that is dominated by men. As educators, it's not our job to fix a student's family life. In this section, we'll focus on the mindsets generated from communities through the lens of cultural competence. In chapter 1, we looked at how the media controls the messages sent to students. In chapter 2, we'll begin by diving into cultural competence to understand where these biases may have originated.

Cultural Competence

In August 2015, the 193 member states of the United Nations came together and created *"Transforming Our World: The 2030 Agenda for Sustainable Development."* This agenda consisted of seventeen sustainable development goals (SDGs). The goals range from ending poverty to climate action, and many others in between. Nestled in one of the top spots (Goal 5) is the goal of gender equality.[26]

Gender equality is an important issue to address throughout the world, from the smallest of towns in the southern states of America to the sub-Saharan African desert. Issues of gender inequality proliferate in communities under a variety of contexts, regardless of where one is geographically located. The goal targets that directly pertain to the issue of achieving gender equity in coding instruction follow:

- End all forms of discrimination against all women and girls everywhere.
- Ensure women's full and effective participation and equal opportunities for leadership at all levels of decision making in political, economic, and public life.
- Enhance the use of enabling technology, in particular information and communications technology, to promote the empowerment of women.
- Adopt and strengthen sound policies and enforceable legislation for the promotion of gender equality and the empowerment of all women and girls at all levels.[27]

"Gender Equality: Why It Matters" states that "disadvantages in education translate into lack of access to skills and limited opportunities in the labour market."[28]

Thus, if the goal is to provide girls with a world of opportunities in a futuristic labor market that has yet to be truly defined (although we know there will be an integration of technology in some way), then education is where we must look to right the wrongs that have been bestowed on our girls. As men and women who work in the field of education, there are a few things we can begin to do right now to address these gender inequalities that exist in education. The report suggests the following (these points are of particular importance and will be addressed in more detail throughout this chapter):

1. *If you are a woman, you can address unconscious biases and implicit associations that can form an unintended and often invisible barrier to equal opportunity.*

2. *If you are a man or a boy, you can work alongside women and girls to achieve gender equality and embrace healthy, respectful relationships.*[29]

Let's look at Bangladesh. In Bangladesh, the labor force participation of rural women is only 36.4 percent compared to 83.3 percent of men.[30] Because the opportunity for education is the largest determinant of an individual's employment opportunity, then it can be assumed that less than one-third of women in the country are receiving proper schooling in their developmental years. Without this proper schooling, the gender disparity within this country will continue to exist. When we layer inequities of the use of technology onto this, then it's clear to see that every piece of progress, no matter how big or small, will have a positive impact on creating more gender equality throughout the industry.

Women in countries like India and Egypt are six times more likely than women in Uganda to say that Internet use is not considered appropriate for them and that their friends or family may disapprove.[31] The more we separate access to these valuable resources, the greater the barrier that girls will need to cross, should they ever decide to pursue a career in computer programming.

In chapter 5, when we look at the "ask three before me" teaching strategy, we'll take a deeper look into the inequalities that exist for young girls around the world and examine ways to create a more balanced learning environment within our own classrooms.

Mansplaining

There's a term that has come to light in the last few years: *mansplaining*. *Merriam-Webster* (*M-W*) dictionary hasn't officially adopted it as of the publication date of this book; however, they have characterized it as one of the words they are watching. In a recent article, *M-W* accurately articulated the term *mansplaining* as something that occurs "when a man talks condescendingly to a woman about something he has incomplete knowledge of, with the mistaken assumption that he knows more about it than the person who he's talking to does."[32]

I bring this up for several reasons.

First, if we're looking to change the culture in our schools to help instill confidence in our young girls, then we must model what that looks like. At educational conferences, I've witnessed mansplaining taking place in interviews and panel discussions. In one interview from 2017, the interviewee was a woman, and the interviewer was a man. As the interviewee (woman) would answer the interviewer's (man's) questions, he would literally restate the interviewee's response in a way that made it seem like it was his idea.

How often does this happen in our schools? In our team meetings?

Some male in a leadership role comes in spewing information about a topic on which he has little or no true knowledge of, just to be the voice, the authority, the (literal) last man standing. When the female starts the conversation on a topic about which she is well versed, the male colleague inserts himself into the discussion by reframing every single word that comes out of the female's mouth.

Now take a look at your classroom.

How often does this happen with your students? Maybe it's during a team project when the boy hogs the stage, showing off "his" ideas that were actually gotten from a girl in his group.

What about the mentor texts we read to our students?

If we're constantly putting females in this box as the supporting characters, or the objects of one's affection, then what message is that conveying to the girls in our classes? We're essentially telling them they should aim low and aspire to be supporting characters, at best. When we suppress the image of females in this way, will they begin to see themselves as the warriors and heroines of their own stories, or will they resign themselves to be one of the small, unnamed characters on the credits at the end of the movie? Which experience do we want for our students?

How Adults Think

In June 2017, I conducted a blind survey at an education conference to capture educators' first instincts of which gender came to their minds when the name of a profession appeared on the screen. With only ten seconds to respond, the educators had to go with their guts and choose the gender they thought of first when they saw each career field. Although a few of the educators in the room were unhappy with this assessment, as they were given only one choice per question, it was important that we conducted this exercise to better understand our own biases. The following are the results of this rapid-fire perspectives survey, with a total of ninety educators participating in this assessment:

Table 2.1: 2017 results from timed survey on gender bias

	Man	Woman	Average Time to Answer (in seconds)
Doctor	61%	39%	5.02
Nurse	6%	94%	3.71
Teacher	10%	90%	3.25
Engineer	72%	18%	3.51

The results are astounding. Practically the same exact gender stereotypes that the media promotes are the ones that are in our minds as adults. Maybe the data represent the physical environment and upbringing of the educator, or maybe it is a better representation of the roles that are projected in the movies and television shows we watch, the music we listen to, or the books we read. Regardless of where these perspectives originate from, it's important that, as educators, we understand our own biases while taking responsibility for the influence they have in our teaching. When we consistently call on the boys in our classes to have them provide input or answer a question related to math and science, then we're sending a subconscious message to the girls in our classes that tells them, "You're not smart enough."

Take a moment to consider your own bias.

What stereotypes do you subscribe to, and how do they influence how you teach or facilitate the learning of the young minds in the room? Has there been a time in your teaching career when a student broke the mold that you placed him or her in? If the mold was broken, what changed in you? In your practice?

Children look up to us as their role models. They follow our thinking and reasoning as a guide for building their own. They seek our wisdom regarding what direction to take. If we are speaking up against gender stereotypes, then so will they. When we challenge outdated ideas of boy-versus-girl behaviors, so will they. And if they see us silently accepting injustices, then guess what they will do…

How Students Think

"It's hard to be something you can't see."—Sheryl Sandberg

Students from as young as four years old tend to answer questions around gender based on the examples they see in their real lives or in the media. If a child has a mother who is a doctor and a father who is a teacher, then that child would be more likely to identify females as doctors and males as teachers. Whereas when you have a child who has a father who works as an engineer and a mother who is a housewife, then that child is likely to see men as engineers and women as housewives.

These close relatives who are related to the child are considered first-tier influencers. Then there are second-tier influencers. Second-tier influencers include real-life people whom the child doesn't necessarily know in person but has seen or interacted with via some form of media. Media include books, magazines, blog posts, radio, TV, film, and the Internet. These second-tier influencers can have a huge impact on the impression that children receive from a very young age. If children are unable to identify with or see role models in their first-tier influencers (parents, guardians, or relatives), then their next look-to is the second-tier influencers of the media.

In the last decade, the media has given us stories that are published based on biases, focusing on the point of view that pays the biggest bucks. They've provided us with "alternative facts," passing them through as full truths. The problem with this equation, with these stories, is that the leading characters in movies and TV shows are typically men, with the woman being cast as a damsel in distress. The more these gender biases persist in the media, the more likely our students are to believe them as the truth, as the way things should be.

The way we combat this is by providing girls with examples of women who are living and succeeding in those areas that are typically dominated by men. In our schools, our elementary classes tend to be heavily populated with women.[33] By the time students enter middle school and high school, they tend to have exposure to more than just one teacher. In the middle-years grade levels, consider who we have in these roles as the math teacher, science teacher, coding teacher, and technology coach. If the ratio is nowhere near 50 percent women in these roles, then it's time that our administrative team takes a step back to investigate why this is the case and what might be done to balance this equation. As tweens become teens, if the only female role models they see in their schools live in the English language arts world, then we are doing them a major disservice by limiting the diversity of perspectives.

If we don't start by looking in our schools first, then how else might we expect to make a real change in society?

It's that simple. If students have real-life role models, even just one who works in a field such as coding or some other technology-based industry, then they are more likely to feel supported in pursuing that field.

The Composition of Our Faculty and Staff
When we look inside the walls of our own schools, what do we see in terms of the gender and ethnicity composition of those individuals who work with our students?

We must take a step back and think about our students.

In their academic careers within the school, will students see someone who looks like them (gender or ethnic or cultural background)?

When they do interact with these professionals, what type of roles are they found in?

How many times throughout children's academic careers will they interact with an adult with whom they can relate to in the diversity sense of the word?

If all our tech teachers, coaches, directors, and IT professionals are white men, then guess what our girls will think? Every school should have strong female role models in the science and technology fields for young girls to connect with and aspire to be like. If they're not seeing these examples in schools, and if they're not seeing these role models in their communities, in movies or in TV shows, then where will they see them?

The composition of our faculty and staff has a huge impact on how students' perspectives are being shaped. If there are no women teaching coding, then guess how likely it would be for a girl to pursue the field of coding? You guessed it: not very.

The faculty and staff of our schools can serve as first-tier influencers for the students we serve. Think about it. How many hours are in a week? 168. How many of those hours are spent at school? 30 to 40. Thus, when you put it all together, the visual impact of educators on a student's life makes up at least 10 to 20 percent. If we count for only the waking hours of the week, subtracting 60 hours from 168, we get 108 hours. If students are in our classes for thirty to forty hours per week, then they are being influenced by us approximately one-third of the time. One-third. Thirty-three percent. That's a hefty piece of the puzzle. The kind of influence that we have within that exposure period will have some type of impact on the students in our care.

Educators have one-third of the influence; parents, caretakers, guardians, and families have one-third of the influence; and the media has the remaining one-third of the influence on our students. There is only one area of influence that we as educators have full control over: ourselves and the environments in which we work.

In part 2 of this book, we'll focus on teaching strategies that have a positive impact on creating a more gender-equitable learning environment for our students.

Gender Stereotypes in Education

In a conversation with a colleague at the start of a recent school year, we talked about classes and the groups of students he had. He taught the physical computing and making course in middle school, and I asked him how many girls he had in his new grade 6 cohort, who were my original students upon coming to this school.

"A lot," he said.

"*You're welcome,*" I wanted to reply.

As we spoke more about his class compositions for his grade-seven and grade-eight cohorts, he told me that the number of girls in those classes was extremely low. Upon prodding further to understand what could have caused the drop in enrollment, I was informed that the girls didn't want to be the only girl in the class.

This is a rampant problem in education. No girl wants to be an island unto herself—nor should she be. As the number of boys enrolling in higher-level courses continues to increase, we must find ways to keep our girls engaged and motivated. In part 3 of this book, we'll look at specific opportunities to use for empowering girls in our learning environments in their quests to learn coding. For now, let's examine our gender stereotypes in education a bit further.

The NPR example in chapter 1 addresses issues that we currently see in education.

A report on the motivation of girls in the area of technology shows that girls as young as six years old subscribe to the stereotype that boys are better at robotics and coding than they are.[34] To overcome this belief, we need to do a better job of highlighting girls' abilities to take risks and problem solve while moving away from the "you're pretty" compliments. Hearing "you're pretty" compliments our outsides. Thus, when we're trying to build up a girl's internal confidence, we need to focus on those internal qualities.

> *"You've been doing a great job on working through this problem. Stick with it. I believe you can solve it."*

This is how you compliment girls' insides. Recognize their resilience, and give them the knowledge that you believe in them. Sometimes in life all we need to hear from another human being is "*I believe in you.*" That statement is often enough to push away our own uncertainties and empower us to once again believe in ourselves.

Bell Schedule Conflicts

The number-one conflict that schools offering a computer-science course in middle or high school have is regarding the issue of bell schedules. Most schools have bell schedules. At some point, typically during middle school or as late as high school years, students get the opportunity to choose which classes they will take. This choice offers a lot of freedom, although I would argue that in most cases, the amount of freedom offered is simply not enough.

Take, for example, a school that heavily promotes world languages and the arts. This school would likely have middle school students take a reading language arts course, a math course, a physical education course, a science course, and a social studies course. The electives students can choose range from choir, band, world language, computer science, or graphic-design classes.

If a student has a passion for the arts, then he or she would be most likely to choose an elective that is arts based. With this choice, the student has filled up his or her six-course schedule, thus throwing the possibility of that computer-science course out the window because the schedule conflict created from choosing that course means that the student will not be able to pursue the arts for which he or she is passionate about.

In talking with a former colleague about the makeup of his classes, he informed me that his coding classes have a combined total of eighty-six boys and nineteen girls. Let's do the math. If my former colleague teaches a total of seven sections of his coding courses, then he would have an average of about twelve boys and two girls in each class. Twelve boys and two girls. And those numbers are only if you're lucky. Often we walk into our coding courses and see the sad story of only one girl in a sea of boys.

We must change this.

In a time where creative solutions to our world's problems are necessary, one would think that schools could stretch their boundaries of possibilities to combine opportunities for students to be creative with opportunities for them to problem solve.

For those school administrators who are reading this right now, take a second look at your course options before they go live. Are we pigeonholing students into a silo-focused career field based on what they choose as their electives? Or are we providing them with the tools they need to create their future career opportunities that are yet to be defined?

The more uniform our schedules look, the less flexibility they tend to possess. When students exit our schools and enter the real world, the rigidness of our spaces and systems will have done very little to prepare them for the flexible spaces they'll have to live, work, and play in.

Historically, girls have had an affinity for the arts.[35] When we look at the images represented in the media, the most well-known artists across industries tend to be women. In our current society, there are women who are integrating their passion for the arts with their computing experience, such as finding ways to make dancers' costumes light up in unison with the beats of a song. This is to say that the integration of arts and computing should not be seen as an impossibility or as something that girls have to choose between before they even become teenagers. By focusing on pairing arts and computing courses rather than pitting them against each other, we're allowing students to discover how their passions could be intertwined instead of having to choose one over the other.

No matter how much we talk about changing a bell schedule or offering more flexibility in course selections, many will still see this as an impossibility. Here's a way to approach this issue from a different lens.

Let's say you have a grade-six student, Becky. Becky wants to take both band and coding, as she has a passion for both subjects. Instead of forcing Becky to choose between (A) band, or (B) coding, why not give her a (C) option? In option C, Becky is provided with the learning standards she must accomplish by the completion of grade six. She is then asked how she would organize her schedule to ensure that these learning standards are accomplished throughout the course of the year. In a time when we should be more focused on empowering our learners rather than dictating to them, getting them to develop creative solutions to a problem allows them to take control of what they learn and how two passions or interests can be integrated with each other, thus making school less of a dictatorship and more of a democratic system.

This C option provides students with agency and a voice that allows them to develop a third option which creatively integrates their passions or interests in a way that links back to the required learning objectives. When students are successful in this third option, they can document it and publish it in a way that shows other students what can be possible as they make their course choices for the following term. When students have a voice in how the hours of their days are spent, they are more likely to be committed to what they are learning rather than just going through the motions.

Gender Stereotypes in Content Areas

When we teach our specific content areas, it is ever so important to be confident in what we're doing. Often in an academic setting, elementary school teachers are charged with teaching math, science, reading, writing, and social studies. In my career as a coach, I have known countless teachers who lacked any type of comfort with teaching such subjects as science and math. They would seek to have a neighboring, often male, teacher handle the science lessons, while the female teacher honed in on the social studies and writing lessons. Doing this is very strategic for the educators involved, but what impact does this swapping have on our students?

Studies conducted on the gender stereotypes in math achievement show that a female teacher's anxiety or uneasiness with math has a significant impact on a female student's math achievement. In a 2009 US study of seventeen grade-one and grade-two teachers, researchers analyzed how the teachers' comfort levels with teaching math would impact the total of fifty-two boys and sixty-five girls in their classes. The study showed that the higher a female teacher's math anxiety, the lower the math achievement was for the female students.[36] Another study, published in 2010, looked at global schools, analyzing the math scores on the PISA and TIMSS assessments. The study found that in countries where there were rampant gender inequities, girls tended to have a lower achievement in math.[37] Thus, our learning environments and the biases or lack of confidence that lives in them has an impact on the ability of our girls to succeed in math achievement. If our perceptions and environments have such an impact on a girl's success in math achievement, then imagine how our uncertainty in other subject areas contributes to a girl's lack of confidence in those content areas.

Girls' Interest in Tech

The thing about girls is that purpose tends to drive their passion. If they are afforded the opportunity to create something that helps someone or something, then they are more likely to stay dedicated to it. Thus, when we frame coding activities around an altruistic purpose, we're more likely to capture the interest of girls and to engage them in this male-dominated field.

In matching altruistic purposes with coding, students of both genders are able to engage in design thinking and collaborative team-building approaches around a common goal.

Work culture tells us that girls will only apply for a job if they are 100 percent sure they can fulfill the job responsibilities, whereas boys will consistently apply for jobs they are unqualified for.

How many times have you pondered over a job opportunity, unsure as to whether you would be able to fulfill the responsibilities?

There is something to be said for the confidence men possess, particularly in the world of tech, compared to the confidence women possess. Men tend to be more fearless, whereas women are more unsure and more cautious so as to not make a mistake. If we're this way in front of our girls, then what message are we sending them?

Part 2

Keys for Gender Equity in Coding

When teaching coding to our students, it is important to focus on the pedagogy. With a content area that is so foreign to so many of us, this section introduces seven keys to help you on your journey. For each key there are tested examples of how the practice works within a learning environment. There will also be an infusion of explicit points made regarding how best to implement these practices in a way that focuses on gender equity in the learning environment. Although this book specifically focuses on coding, my hope is that you will find that these teaching practices can work across many content areas, especially because coding and technology are two areas that shouldn't be seen as silos (with the exception of computer science in high school environments, where the computer-science principles are offered as an advanced-placement test).

Seven Keys for Achieving Gender Equity in Teaching Coding:

1. Get frustrated
2. Adopt the iteration mind-set
3. Ask three before me
4. Utilize pair programming
5. Allow the student to become the expert
6. Complete the lesson first
7. Reflecting and learning keywords

Get Frustrated

You're human, right? If you answered yes, then you know as well as I do that as humans we make mistakes. Things that we may not understand often frustrate us. Showing your students that you are human allows them to relate to you. When they see how you react to challenges, they'll begin to follow suit. With frustration being a part of the human condition, we as educators would do well to learn a thing or two about how to handle our frustrations. Sometimes this can be related to emotional intelligence. Thinking of our youngest learners, though, we can't expect them to enter our classes with a single iota of understanding of their own emotional intelligence. Our intention in this chapter is not to teach didactic emotional intelligence. Rather, it is to recognize that the learning process in a new endeavor like coding will be frustrating and that there are healthy ways for us to model frustration for the benefit of our students, thereby creating an equitable learning environment.

In my worldly travels, I have been frustrated many times. For example, during a recent trip when I traveled alone to China, I became frustrated when my taxi driver got lost while taking me an hour and a half away from the city to my rather remote hotel near a popular tourist destination. The driver only spoke Chinese, and I only spoke English. His speech came across as yelling, with the tone and pitch he displayed frustrating me to no end. Coupling his tone and pitch with the language barrier, I was stuck. This was a communication barrier, and aside from showing him the Google Maps directions of where to take me, I was lost, both communicatively and directionally. Understanding the root of my frustration, I was able to breathe and in a relatively calm state redirect the driver by pointing in the way of the directions that the map was showing me. As it turned out, we were a lot closer to the hotel than it had seemed.

    I could have told the taxi driver to let me out of the taxi so that I could finish getting to my destination by foot (as I've done before in cities that I was familiar with), or I could have stayed and been patient with the experience as we collaboratively figured out how to overcome the language barrier. I chose to stay. I chose to persist through the barriers. In doing so, we made a U-turn that allowed me to see the sign for my hotel as well as some fellow foreign travelers who confirmed the hotel's location long before it got dark.

As educators, we have an intrinsic expectation to know all the answers. We expect to be right all the time. These expectations are unrealistic in a day and age when historic "facts" are being disproved. Pluto is not a planet. The real computers behind NASA's first space launch were Black women. With all the new technologies that are being developed and implemented in modern education, we have answers to our learners' questions at our fingertips. Sometimes the answers we find are incorrect, if we even find them at all.

When a lesson goes south, what do we do?

Our students will reciprocate the way in which we show our frustrations. Remember, we are the ones who they look up to. If we never show them what it's like to get frustrated, then they're likely to internalize their frustration as something that is abnormal or unhealthy, thereby exhibiting the very behaviors that would get them sent to the principal's office for disciplinary actions or get them kicked out of school.

My first year teaching, I had a little boy named Christopher in my daily morning reading intervention group. Christopher had a challenging home life and would literally *run* from the things that frustrated him, turning the learning environment into a game of cat and mouse. Having very little training at the time, I had no idea how to get Christopher to sit still. For the first few days, I played into his game, chasing after him and leaving the other sixteen students to read silently, as I thought that his wrangling was my responsibility. One day I decided that enough was enough. After witnessing Christopher get up and run away at the same moment every morning, I had an "aha" moment. Christopher was acting up at the point in the round-robin reading when he didn't know how to pronounce a word. Instead of trying to pronounce the word as the other students did, Christopher would run away from the challenge.

[There's an old saying from Abraham Lincoln that goes, *"Better to remain silent and thought a fool than to speak out and remove all doubt."* For our kids who are silent or who run away from intellectually challenging learning opportunities, I tend to wonder if this quote was repeated in their bedtime stories.]

I decided to do a little role-playing to see if it would encourage Christopher to stay.

The next morning, I started the round-robin reading. At a certain point in the text, I "accidentally" stumbled on the word *decision*. I stopped and said out loud, "Wait, that didn't sound right." Going back to the word, I asked the group of students for some help in sounding out the word *decision*. The first time, I had pronounced it "*deck-is-i-o-n*." When I opened it up to the students to help me with the proper pronunciation, they were able to *teach me* the proper pronunciation of "dee-si-zion" without poking fun at me. During this exercise, Christopher was an observer. He watched as the other students helped me pronounce the word. He witnessed as nobody laughed. It was at this moment that Christopher was able to see how helpful the students were when one of their fellow learners got frustrated from a mistake that he or she made or, in this case, a word that he or she couldn't pronounce properly on the first try.

From that pivotal moment onward, I began to see a change in Christopher. We stopped playing cat and mouse, and he began to let his guard down in learning from and with the other students in the group.

When we're using technology in the classroom, this is likely the easiest way to show students exactly what it looks like to get frustrated. The interactive whiteboard doesn't work, the app won't open, the Internet is down—you name it, it happens. When we experience these frustrating happenings as educators, it becomes increasingly important for us to demonstrate what this frustration looks like.

Never should there be a time when we utter the words "I'm just not good at tech." This statement is crippling not only for ourselves as educators but also for the students who hear us say it. As soon as we put ourselves down by saying that we're not good at something, we create an immediate handicap. This disability might have begun in our minds, but now that the words have been spoken aloud, we wear them as a tattoo directly on our faces for all to see. By claiming that we're not good enough, we are creating a climate in which learning potential is limited.

I can't begin to tell you how many classrooms I've been in as a coach when I've had to outright correct the portrait that a teacher was creating of him- or herself. As educators, we should not be throwing in the towel when we face challenges. When we encounter something that lives outside of our wheelhouse of expertise, let's begin adding the word *yet* to that initial negative statement. "*I'm not good at tech yet*," sounds much more positive than "*I'm not good at tech*." The word *yet* adds a futuristic tense of possibility, preventing the shattering of hope. What's even better is that when our students hear us transforming these originally negative statements into positive, hopeful opportunities with the addition of the word *yet*, they become more likely to add it to the end of their own negative statements as well.

If students aren't catching the drift, then a little nudge or friendly reminder that "*we don't use negative talk like that in this class*" will surely get the students to better understand and adjust their words, thereby adding positive value to their perspectives.

Getting back to the tech not working.

The computer won't turn on. Do you pick it up and throw it across the room? Do you curse at it? Do you smack it around? Sure, we all think these things in our Ally McBeal[38] minds, but in reality, what do we do?

There are multiple correct solutions for dealing with these frustrating situations. We could give the device a break and step away from it for a little while. (*Note: "a little while" does not mean multiple hours, days, weeks, or months.*)

What's even better is to frame this break in terms of a quantity of time: "After we finish this lesson, I'll try to fix it as you all read silently," or "We'll come back to this after recess." By announcing that you're putting a set amount of time between you and the problem, you're modeling an effective way for students to approach the frustration that *will* occur as they enter the world of computational thinking through problem solving.

Another great approach to use in modeling effective frustration is by turning it into a collaborative inquiry. As the teacher, you're not the only human in the room. You likely have a roomful of twenty to thirty smaller humans. Why not state your problem to the class and ask them how they would pursue the solution? Often students will surprise us by coming up with a creative working solution that we never even considered. By turning your frustration into a collaborative inquiry, you are helping students realize the power of working interdependently with others.

Here are some examples of negative and positive ways to show frustration:

Negative	**Positive**
• Throw a fit • Throw a device • Throw a temper tantrum • Curse	✓ Take a break from the situation ✓ Verbalize your troubleshooting process ✓ Ask for help ✓ Breathe

The Impact Frustration Has on Girls

When it comes to getting frustrated, I've noticed that my female students exhibit this a bit differently than the male students did. While working at an all-girls school in Washington, DC, I initiated our Blogging Club and transformed it into a Coding Club to give the girls a greater challenge in critical thinking and problem solving. The club was open to girls in grades two through five. Although the composition was of girls from different grade levels, they all supported one another equally. One of the girls, Beatrice, a second grader, had a challenging time with this new club. This was her (and all the girls') first experience with coding. Beatrice was accustomed to getting all the right answers in school. She made the honor roll every term and consistently received the highest accolades in her grade level. When it came to coding, Beatrice got frustrated very early on. Things weren't coming to her as quickly as she had hoped. She was struggling and didn't know how to cope.

In our very first session, about fifteen minutes into the activity, Beatrice hid under a computer desk and began to cry. I went over and asked her what was wrong. She refused to speak for a solid ten minutes as she huddled in a ball, drowning in her own tears of frustration. Once she was able to gain the slightest amount of composure, she told me that she was stuck. You see, Beatrice had never not known the answer to a problem. Up until this point, she had never truly experienced frustration, so she didn't know how to handle this new emotion. It's kind of like the movie *Inside Out*[39] when Riley's emotions get all jumbled up, causing her to act out in ways she never had before.

Beatrice's reaction is one that some girls have when they first begin learning how to code. Although she retreated into a ball of tears, some girls decide to just walk away and never return altogether. The only way to mitigate this from having such an everlasting effect is to model what frustration looks like and to show students that it is perfectly OK if they don't get the correct answer right away—reiterating that failing is a part of learning.

In working with girls, we must show them ways in which to be productively frustrated and how to get beyond that frustration. In another environment, a girl in my Girls Coding Club got frustrated with the program she was working on. She scooted her chair back, crossed her arms, and refused to work on the program, stating that it was "too hard." When I went to investigate what was happening with her, I noticed that her screen was blank. She had deleted all the code she had created. It's OK to feel frustrated in this way. As educators, we must validate this feeling because it is exactly that—a feeling. While we validate the emotion, we should also be providing students with strategies for overcoming their frustrations.

Allow a moment for the frustration to be felt, then through questioning, guide the student through finding the logical steps that he/she would need to take to solve the problem. You could even team up with the student and laugh at the problem. Make fun of the computer; tell it, "Listen to me." Then, as the student works to solve the problem, she'll realize that she has the power to control both the computer and her own emotions.

The book *Hello Ruby* mentioned in chapter 1 perfectly models the frustration and thought process of computational thinking. Reading this book to girls gives them a perspective of how they might overcome their frustrations with a program. Our girls need to know that it is OK to not be perfect with every new endeavor they undertake.

Social emotional learning is a cornerstone within a child's academic development. When we get students to become aware of the causes of their emotions, they are better able to manage both their emotions and their actions that accompany those emotions. The ability to live in the ambiguity that comes with learning how to code allows students to develop resilience in their practice, focusing more on the process rather than on being glued to the solution itself. It is here, in this ambiguous discomfort, that students can truly understand the emotions that bubble up as they experience these frustrating trials and tribulations that come with learning how to code.

One final tip to keep in mind when we're modeling frustration for our young girls is to be aware of who we default to for help. Consistently calling on someone to fix all tech problems, before you take the time to troubleshoot them yourself, sends the message to girls that they're simply not smart enough to even consider taking on such a task or solving such a problem. The marketing world has had an impact on the rectification of this confidence problem in the last decade. Take the example of Barbie's response in 2013 (also expounded upon previously in chapter 1). Do a simple Google search on "Barbie book for coding," and you'll undoubtedly come across the stream of articles written about how *Barbie: I Can Be a Computer Engineer* sends the message to girls that if they want to learn how to code, then they should ask a boy. Although they've since created new books and movies to promote girls in their coding journeys, that first published book illustrating the damsel-in-distress Barbie getting a boy to create programs for her and fix her code will be sketched into Mattel's "Wall of Oops," for a long time to come.

The next time you get frustrated with something in your classroom, take the time to live collaboratively in the frustration with your students. Don't just jump on the phone and call someone to come and solve the problem. And if you have a woman who works in your school within IT or in some other tech-based role, then try giving her a call to help out rather than consistently defaulting to the man in the office.

Adopt the Iteration Mind-Set

It's curious that we spend more time congratulating people who have succeeded than encouraging people who have not.
—Neil DeGrasse Tyson

Life is all about learning how to persevere, about learning how to learn. It's OK to make mistakes. We should be teaching our students how to learn from their mistakes rather than throwing in the towel after defeats. Iteration focuses on resilience in the face of defeat.

> *Iteration: The act of repeating a process either to generate an unbounded sequence of outcomes or with the aim of approaching a desired goal, target, or result.*[40]

Myrtle Urkel exemplifies an iteration mind-set when she approaches Eddie Winslow to be her love quest in the 1980s US sitcom *Family Matters*[41]. From Myrtle's introduction into the show, she instantly sees Eddie Winslow as her love interest.

Episode after episode shows the geeky Myrtle, cousin to the even geekier Steve Urkel, attempting to win the heart of one Eddie Winslow. She tries flirting, giving him gifts, climbing trees—literally anything she can to get his attention.

When her first attempt wasn't accepted, she persisted. She iterated. She continued forward in pursuit of her goal with one vision in mind—to win the heart of Eddie Winslow. The only changing variable in this example was in the variety of attempts that Myrtle took in how she approached Steve. Had she given up after her first unsuccessful attempt, the story line would have sadly ended, unfulfilled.

Iteration is a learning opportunity that is easier said than done. When we are iterating, we have an idea in mind of where we want to be, but we're not quite sure of how to get there. We may try the same approach repeatedly, editing our initial decisions as we come face-to-face with obstacles. These obstacles get us to analyze our actions to see how best we might adjust our path. As the saying goes, "When the going gets tough, the tough get going." This is not the same as saying that the tough leave, but rather that the tough continue steadfastly working toward their goals.

The thing about an iteration mind-set is that we need to be encouraging students to adopt this as part of their learning profiles. Some call it grit, while others call it resilience or perseverance. Iteration is more of a combination of grit, perseverance, and resilience, with a large scoop of computational thinking.

There is an adage that says, "If at first you don't succeed, try, try again." But when do we know when to change paths altogether?

That's easy.

Take my driver's education experience, for example.

I took driver's education at the tender age of sixteen. Back then, there was a written test and a driving test. In order to take either part of the test, you had to spend thirty hours driving with a licensed driver. My licensed driver was my dad, and the vehicle was his pickup truck. Overall, the whole driving part was easy, minus the steering and turning parts. It was the parallel parking and the three-point turns that held me back the most. Neither my parallel parking nor my three-point turns were ever perfect, but being the anxious teenager that I was, I convinced my dad to let me take the driving test.

The written test was easy; however, shortly after getting behind the wheel of the driver's education car, my driving supervisor told me to make a three-point turn. That three-point turn quickly became a twenty-one-point turn, and at that moment, I had failed the test.

With that first failure, I could have just thrown in the towel altogether, resigned to live at home with Mom and Dad for the rest of my life, ride my bicycle everywhere, and become a hermit. I took one look at the future, with big alligator tears of fear in my eyes, and decided to attempt to pass the test yet again.

My dad took me under his wing once more. After weeks of driving practice, I still wasn't getting the hang of the three-point turn. But I was making some progress. My twenty-one-point turn had become a fifteen-point turn. I thought maybe, just maybe, I could take the driving test again and actually pass this time. Two weeks after my first fail, we went back to the driver's education office so that I could take the driving test again. I had already passed the written test, so now I was only required to pass the driving portion. When I got into the driver's seat, I took a deep breath. I knew where my trouble points were, and I was one step closer to knowing how to solve them. When the instructor asked me to do a three-point turn, I gave it my best shot. This time around, as in my practice sessions, my twenty-one-point turn had become a fifteen-point turn.

I was crushed.

It was as though my life depended on this driving test. How many times would I be allowed to fail the test? What if I never passed?

My parents pointed out that this time I had made some significant progress, and they had faith that I would get my driver's license. They believed in me when my own confidence was shaken.

> *As educators, sometimes we'll need to be that support system for the students in our care when they lack faith in themselves.*

I wasn't ready to throw in the towel just yet. It was as though I was looking into a magic ball that showed me the kind of life that I'd have if I just gave up altogether—and I didn't like what I saw. My dad, the patient man he was, took me under his wing one more time. This time we practiced driving in a car, instead of his hard-to-turn pickup truck. What a difference the car made! After watching my dad do the three-point turn (from outside the vehicle) and seeing which way the tires went as he turned the wheel in different directions, I was better able to understand the mechanics of the car. When he had me get into the driver's seat to try it myself, I breathed life into the verbalization of each step, saying my moves out loud before I completed them. I had never done this before. Having previously navigated off of a false sense of confidence (also known as cockiness), this time was new, as I was able to verbally describe what the car was doing as I completed the three-point turn. After three weeks of practice, I was finally able to master the three-point turn in the car with my dad.

Now it was time to prove my chops by taking the driving test one more time. If I didn't pass it this time, I'd likely cry and then proceed to practice and take the test again. If I did pass it, I'd still cry, but they'd be tears of happiness, the ones that don't even touch your face as they fly from your eyes.

The instructor and I got into the driver's education vehicle. He directed me to make a three-point turn. I mumbled the directions to myself as I turned the wheel in the correct directions. One. Two. Three. I had *finally* made a three-point turn!

The moral of this story is very simple.

Iteration is the key to success.

Sometimes students will need to physically walk through the steps of a problem. Sometimes they might need to plot it out on a piece of paper. Sometimes they'll need to read it out as though it were a story unfolding.

My pinned tweet for the last few years reads:

Tara Linney
@TaraLinney

Turning education into iteration w/o fearing failure #moonshotthinking #gafesummit

9:02 PM · 20 Jul 2014

This mantra is one that we should be fostering in education. Too often when students get something wrong, they throw in the towel and quit, assuming that their lack of understanding means that they don't fit and never will. We need to help them see past this.

The ISTE Student Standard: Innovative Designer 4D states that students "exhibit a tolerance for ambiguity, perseverance and the capacity to work with open-ended problems."[42] In coding, there are a variety of ways in which a problem can be approached. Typically, when students enter into coding for the first time, there are many elements to the program with which they are unfamiliar. Just because a learner is unfamiliar with something doesn't mean that he or she should shy away from the challenging scenario. When Amelia Earhart set out to make the first flight around the world, she was encountering unchartered territory. No one had done this before. Ambiguity was at an all-time high. If the plane hadn't made it off the ground, do you think she would have thrown in the towel and given up?

If all the world's inventors had given up on their first attempts, then we wouldn't have cures for pneumonia, motor vehicles wouldn't exist, the Internet would have never become a thing, and globalization would have never been born. This is not the world that a good percentage of the population currently lives in. We have found and are finding cures for deadly diseases, and we are improving the lives of our neighbors and ourselves. When Google first developed Google Glass, their design was flawed to the point of being un-wearable to the general public due to its aesthetic distaste. Through a series of iterations[43], Google was able to develop an Explorer version of Google Glass for early adopters that initially sold for $2,000, bringing their most viable product to market, and later personalizing it from a consumer product to one that benefited doctors and other professionals.

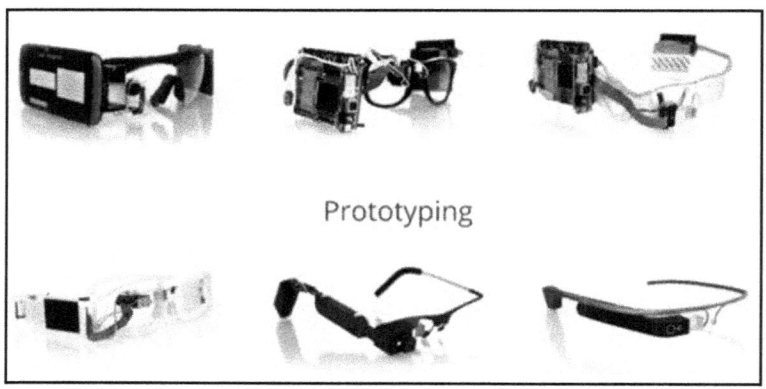

Figure 4.1: Google Glass iterations

We often learn the most from the experiences that we find the most challenging, the most uncomfortable. Staying in one place makes us stagnant. We get complacent, and we may even get so comfortable with the consistency of it all that we refuse to stretch, we fail to dream, and we limit ourselves from imagining the possibilities of what could be.

Exhibiting a tolerance for ambiguity allows us as humans to inquire into the possibilities for solutions to problems that are open-ended. If we can get comfortable in the uncomfortable elements of knowledge acquisition, then we can more fully adopt an iteration mind-set that enables us to learn and grow through challenges by focusing on the process.

As the lead learner in teaching students how to code, I operate as the lead inquirer, helping students solve their problems through a series of appropriately spaced strategic questions. In helping through questioning, we are teaching students what it's like to be problem solvers and what it's like to iterate.

With coding, like with math, science, reading, and writing, we have preconceived assumptions about who will understand the best and the fastest. But what if we are wrong?

In building an iteration mind-set, would you assume that the high-flying students would be able to adapt more quickly than the low flyers? If your vote was for the high flyers, then you might be wrong. High-performing students have their sights set on being high-performing. They don't set out to just pass, to barely scrape by. Their eye is on the highest prize, whether that be an A on a test or first place in a race. When they cannot attain this high level of success, they see it as a failure (re: Jessie Spano on *Saved by the Bell*[44] singing "I'm So Excited"). The whole mantra of "failure is not an option" (famous words from Gene Kranz in regard to the Apollo 13 space mission) has likely been ingrained in these high flyers for the bulk of their lives. When they come face-to-face with failure, they're unable to call on their resilience to help them bounce back, to iterate.

Low-performing students, on the other hand, have iteration ingrained into who they are as learners. Things don't come easy to them, so when they fail, they're already used to it. Some of the best coding students I've ever had were ones who had an individualized education plan or a language barrier, were English-as-a-second-language students, or weren't on their current grade's reading level. Day in and day out, they hit roadblocks in their learning. But they persist. They fail a test, but they see the light at the end of the tunnel, as that score of a 59 is still higher than the 32 they earned the week before. They get stuck on the pronunciation of a word, so they go back and sound it out over and over again until it makes sense to them. When these "low-performing" students are introduced to coding for the first time, it magically seems to just click. Coding is not about having the right answer, as our high-performing students are accustomed to, but about understanding the process.

When we get students to take the time to look at their process and to examine each step as though it's part of a sequential story, we're building up their ability to iterate. Keeping in mind the idiom of *"If at first you don't succeed, try, try again."*

Regardless of how or why students are the lowest achievers, there tends to be one common thread: failure is an option. These students have been failed by our schools and by our systems time and time again. The one teaching practice that we deployed on them over and over again hasn't stuck. We've tried to use manipulatives—nothing. We've given modified tests and homework assignments—nothing.

These students, the castaways of education, are the ones who have the greatest natural success with coding. The logic here is simple, really. These students have grown so used to failing or being failed by the education system that iteration becomes a part of who they are. It is ingrained into their makeup. When they face these failed attempts in learning coding, they already half expect to fail based on previous experience. Thus, when they do fail, they get right back up on the horse and try again. Why? Because it's ingrained in them, it is what they know how to do. They live in a world where they're constantly wrong, so when they get a solution wrong, it's nothing new; it's not a shock.

Conversely, when we're working with these students and they experience success, we need to be there for them emotionally when they experience these triumphs. After being castaways in the academic world for so long, these low-level academic performers may be so jaded that they don't realize success when it happens to them.

Coupling this with girls' already low confidence in the fields of math, science, and technology, we may see a cataclysmic meltdown because success is something they never imagined in multiple parts of their identities within the learning environment.

The ISTE Student Standard: Computational Thinker indicates that students will "develop and employ strategies for understanding and solving problems in ways that leverage the power of technological methods to develop and test solutions."[45] This standard exemplifies the ways in which students should be approaching problem solving.

The ISTE Student Standard: Innovative Designer 4D states that "students exhibit a tolerance for ambiguity, perseverance and the capacity to work with open-ended problems."[46] The keyword here is *ambiguity*, as it means comfort with the unknown or uncertainty. To be an effective problem-solver, students need to get comfortable with the unknown, not complacent. Comfort means that one has the ability to live in a space without freaking out. Complacency, on the other hand, has more to do with being happy or proud in an environment.

To grow, we must find comfort in the unknown, not run away from the things that terrify us.

Remember Beatrice from the previous chapter on frustration?

Beatrice was always a high flyer, so when she faced learning challenges—that's just it, she didn't face learning challenges. When she faced challenges in learning coding, her immediate response was to run away and hide. She thought that failure meant that this would be something she would never succeed in learning.

To help students embrace this iteration mind-set, get them out of their seats and playing out the steps of their programs in the physical world through movement, or have them sketch out the paths they will try next.

In creating an equitable environment in coding, especially in supporting girls with this endeavor, an iteration mind-set is necessary. Coding is not something we achieve overnight. Having multiple opportunities to reach a goal is a must. Even setting the goal as a number of unique attempts rather than finishing a program or obtaining some prize at the end in OK. The important thing here is that we empower students to reflect on their process. This is how the iterative mind-set will help learners of all backgrounds be successful in learning how to code.

Ask Three before Me

Incorporating the teaching tool "ask three before me" is about having students ask others for assistance—taking the pressure off of you. It encourages learners to become *interdependent* on one another instead of independent of.

When I began teaching, I also began indulging in a nightly glass of wine after a long day's work. It's a profession-based thing, as I was not much of a wino when I worked in the nonprofit and marketing worlds. We all have our vices and our reasons for those vices. The reason for my drinking in this profession was quite simple—I was spending *every day* answering the same question from my little eight- and nine-year-olds at least twenty-six times (which is crazy because we only had twenty-three students!).

I was not behaving as a teacher. I was instead operating as an enabler—and not the good type.

In modern education, we need to move out of the enabler role and pivot into the empowerment role, encouraging our students to connect more with others. In Future Work Skills research, the number two skill in the "10 Skills for the Future Workforce" is social intelligence.[47] If we're truly getting students ready for their future work lives, then it's part of our job to help them build a level of social intelligence. Social intelligence is the ability to connect to others in a deep and direct way, to sense and simulate reactions and desired interactions. When we incorporate the *"ask three before me"* strategy into our teaching practice, we're getting students to open up and interact with one another instead of immediately defaulting to the adult in the room for instructions, answers, or support. In these interactions with others, students need to be aware of their own interactions, as well as those of others when they are asking for assistance.

Cultural Competence

One of the ISTE Standards for Educators centers on cultural competency. Collaborator Standard 4D states that educators will "demonstrate cultural competency when communicating with students, parents and colleagues, and interact with them as co-collaborators in student learning." The standard highlights cultural competency as "being able to interact appropriately and effectively with people from other cultures. Being mindful of others' experiences and aware of one's own identity and ideas about difference." The standard describes "interact with them as co-collaborators in student learning" as meaning that "cultural competency takes the experience and identities of all parties as a sign of the uniqueness of each class and of each student. Thoughtfulness in designing learning experiences that consider cultural identities can enhance student learning and improve collaboration and communication with parents or guardians and other stakeholders."[48]

Third-Culture Kids

It is important to understand the cultural competence that is integrated into these interactions that students have with one another when we incorporate "*ask three before me*" into our teaching practice. In some cases, students from different cultural backgrounds may look at asking others for assistance as a sign of weakness. Take, for example, students who are third-culture kids (TCKs). These students (1) have one or both parents who possess one cultural background, (2) the student himself or herself was born or has a passport from a different country than that of his or her parent(s), and (3) the student may be living in a different country than that of the first two identifiers altogether. The term *third-culture kid* tends to relate to a student's formative years, although adults can also fit into this category. With the corporate world becoming so globalized in the last forty years, we are likely to see a proliferation of TCKs in our schools, particularly if we are working within private or international schools, where the admission of students is like a revolving door. As families leave a country in December, we see new families entering our schools for the first time in January. Depending on the country, this revolving-door practice may take place quarterly or year-round.

When we receive these TCKs into our classrooms, it's important to understand the whole child and his or her cultural background. This includes getting beyond the basic question of "Where are you from?" as this is a question that is not easily answered by the TCK population. Give these students the time and space to adjust to the classroom environment. They may not quickly identify with a culture that matches their own; however, from their worldly travels, they tend to have an easier time developing friendships with others from different cultures. Although these students may be some of the most tolerant ones in a class, it's important that other students learn to be tolerant of the cultural ambiguity of the TCK as well. Take the time to allow students to learn about one another, building a classroom culture that fosters the acceptance of differences.

Military Brats

Then you have a more nationalized version of the TCK, which is popular in the United States, where children are military brats. The term *military brat* is used to define a child who has lived in one or more countries or cities because of his or her parents' military occupation. In this context, the term *brat* is seen as a term of endearment, not one of disparagement.

I am a military brat. My parents met in the coast guard in the 1970s. My mother was born and raised in Wisconsin, while my father was born and raised in New Jersey and Pennsylvania. Within my childhood years, we tended to move an average of every two to four years. My older brother was born in New Jersey. I was born in Connecticut. We moved to North Carolina when I was two years old and then to New Jersey when I was six. (I still remember trying to dig a hole from New Jersey to China.) When I was seven years old, we moved back to North Carolina. Then, when I was nine years old, we moved to California. My dad retired from the coast guard when I was in the fifth grade, just before I turned eleven, and because my mom had a job waiting for her back in North Carolina, my parents decided to retire there. My brother and I were pulled out of school a couple of months before the school year ended. My mom homeschooled my brother and I for those last two months as we drove cross-country from California to Florida, where we stayed with my paternal grandparents until our new house was built in North Carolina.

As a biracial (part Caucasian, part Black) girl, I fit in seamlessly while we were in California, as I knew the predominant language (Spanish) from my younger years of schooling, and my skin complexion was similar to that of most of my fellow classmates'.

The small town that we ended up in when we arrived in North Carolina was the polar opposite of what we had experienced in California. Back then, in the mid-1990s, my brother and I were the only biracial people in a town with a population of two thousand people. This created an isolation complex of not fitting in within the environment. It was the worst type of bullying—pure exclusion for being different and having a firm Valley Girl accent. Friends were not easy to come by, and so when it came to ask three before me, I would have rarely ever been among the three who were asked. Even though I had literally just come from a school in California where I placed second in a regional competition similar to the modern-day math Olympiads - my new classmates didn't care. I was judged by my teachers based on my grades and merit, and I was judged by my classmates based on the color of my skin and my accent.

With this experience, I'm able to work with students to ensure that there is more diversity in the perspectives and assistance they seek from their fellow classmates. This diversity includes their interactions with other genders as well as the interactions they have with students of other cultures who don't look the same as everyone else in the room. It's no fun being the odd one out. As educators, we need to be aware of this, working to create a more equitable learning environment for all of our learners, not just zoning in on the majority, or the middle.

Global Gender Inequities

As the civilizations of our world continue to undergo devastation from natural disasters, political turmoil, wars, and conflicts among groups of people, we are likely to see more young students coming into our schools to take refuge in a safe haven to pursue opportunities that may be forbidden in their native countries. Welcoming these students into our learning environments is a highly important undertaking if we are going to provide more opportunities for gender equity in coding education. Goal five of the sustainable development goals, gender equality, sets out to "achieve gender equality and empower all women and girls."[49] To achieve this in our classrooms, we must examine some of the major global stigmas surrounding girls and education.

Looking at the long-standing female infanticide example of the People's Republic of China, as well as several other countries around the world, we're able to see why the girls from these cultural backgrounds may be closed off or more reserved when they enter our classes. The boys in parts of China are often referred to as a "Prince," as it is they who carry on the family name. Although Chinese girls may be some of the smartest students in the class, their cultural background displaces them as "the unwanted ones." The more we perpetuate this belief, the harder it will be for these girls to overcome obstacles and the less likely they will be to find their voices.

Sixty-two million girls are not in school today, and sixteen million of those girls will never start school.[50] With the sheer number of girls who will never start school being twice that of the boys who will go to school, we need to pay better attention to the girls who do make their way into our classrooms. They could very well be the first females in their families to attend school or to matriculate through the entirety of an educational program. Thus, care needs to be taken to ensure that their voices and their confidence are not crippled before they have the chance to blossom.

In respecting the cultures of others, we must find ways to balance this with our school and classroom cultures to ensure that students have an equitable opportunity for success as they enter a new learning environment.

The Quiet Ones

We mustn't forget about our quietest students. Some may be quiet because of confidence, others because of culture, and others just because it's their personality. Regardless of the reason for their quiet demeanor, we need to ensure that the quiet ones don't become the forgotten ones. As you walk around the room to observe students working on their programs, pay special attention to your quietest students.

Are they advancing through the creation of a program, understanding how they've reached each success?

When other students get stuck at red lights, are these quiet students zooming through all the green ones?

Before putting these quiet students on the spot and directing others to them, you may need to build up their confidence by complimenting their process. Once you've managed to crack a smile out of these students, or some other form of positive affirmation, you've got an opportunity to get them to support others. First, encourage the quiet ones to help others when a fellow classmate asks for assistance. Then, you may need to prompt a student who requires help to go to that quiet student. If the quiet student was able to walk you through his or her problem-solving process, then he or she will be able to support a fellow classmate through this process with the right type of ushering and support from you as the teacher.

The 4Cs

Having students *"ask three before me"* also supports the 4Cs in education: communication, collaboration, critical thinking, and creativity.[51] When students are empowered to ask others for help, they are building their ability to communicate with others. They are also building their speaking language in regard to computing languages. Students quickly learn from their communication with one another that they can't simply say, "I want this to go there." Those who help the student with this problem would ask the student to explain his or her question in a more coherent way. The three who are helping the student also build their language because they can't just take over. Rather, they need to work on their communication skills, explaining or inquiring about what the other student should be doing in order to make the code work.

One important point here is that you want to be sure to remind students that when they are helping one another, then they are not using their hands. They must use their words. When students want to help one another, often we see that the helper takes over for the student needing help. We need to remind students that taking over doesn't actually teach the other student anything.

What happens the next time they get stuck in a similar position?

"*Ask three before me*" is a teaching habit for coding that works across all age levels of students. Although this may be something that is asked of students when they are in elementary school, this is an expectation that we can remind them of when they are in high school and beyond. The ISTE Student Standard: Empowered Learner states "students leverage technology to take an active role in choosing, achieving and demonstrating competency in their learning goals, informed by the learning sciences." Looking specifically at standard 1B, "Students build networks and customize their learning environments in ways that support the learning process."[52] In "*ask three before me*", students can be empowered to create physical and virtual networks of experts from diverse backgrounds, keeping track of how a classmate helped them and jotting down notes about the type of service and collaboration they received to more easily recall who to seek out when they encounter future problems. If boys stick with boys and girls stick with girls, then neither gender will benefit from a diverse portfolio of potential collaborators.

By fostering the 4Cs in learning coding, we are encouraging students to build on their language ability as well as their computational thinking, which is related to critical thinking. Computational thinking is the thought process involved in formulating a problem and expressing its solutions in a way that can effectively be carried out to successful completion.[53]

We need to remember our girls when incorporating this *"Ask 3, before me"* practice into coding.

When Johnny gets stuck in a coding activity, and you tell him to ask three before me, there is a high probability that he will respond, "I did." Don't let the interaction stop there. Ask Johnny who he asked. When he lists the names of three boys, redirect him to ask a girl. In our ingrained gender roles, we tend to stick with what's familiar. If we're a girl who gets stuck, then we ask another girl for help. If we're a boy who gets stuck, then we ask another boy for help. We need to get beyond this. Part of building up girls' empowerment in the area of coding is reminding them that they are smart and asking them to share their intelligence in an area where their classmates are stuck. Just like in the 2016 hit movie *Hidden Figures*,[54] the answers are all there, but are we involving the right people in the creation of the solutions?

In April 2016, the Advertising Standards Authority in London began its draft of new advertising rules that would eliminate gender roles in the media.[55] After ads depicting a little boy growing up to be a mathematician and a little girl growing up to be a ballerina, London decided that enough was enough. Understanding the impact that the media has on one's decisions in life, we must take a more active step in education to help students see that they can be anything they set their minds to. We need to show them examples of women who've been successful in science and men who've been successful in fashion. Only when they see people who look like them in varied career roles will they begin to think they can pursue those passions and careers that live within them too.

The next time students get stuck in a coding activity, let's remind them to ask for assistance from someone they've never asked before. Let's tell them to ask a girl.

Utilize Pair Programming

When flagging down a taxi to take me home from work, I've learned to not give my address. It's not that I'm concerned about stalkers or anything like that. For the last couple of years, I've lived in Singapore, one of the world's smallest countries. Small countries are anything but stagnant. With new building developments popping up every month or so, I've learned to say one simple thing to taxi drivers: "*Jackson Square.*" Jackson Square is a sixty-year-old business located in Toa Payoh. It is almost as old as the country itself, and it is a short walk from where I live. Rather than telling the driver the name of my condo, I have learned that simply saying "Jackson Square" gets the driver going in the right direction without me losing my cool. As the driver gets close to Jackson Square, I'm able to tell him or her to keep going straight and to drop me off at the condo on the left.

Simple instructions. Much simpler than guiding the driver through every twist and turn. The beauty of this is that I never have the urge to take the wheel. I simply give a landmark, paying attention as the driver gets to where he or she knows where to go. Then when we're within a few kilometers of Jackson Square, I verbally guide the driver to my final destination.

Pair programming is very similar to this. In pair programming, two students practice computing on one device. Student A operates as the driver, while student B operates as the navigator. The purpose of pair programming is to eliminate the chance of bugs or mistakes within a program. Utilizing pair programming allows the programmers to modify a program, iterating or innovating it as needed to meet a specific goal or need.

In a car, you have the passenger and you have the driver. Now let's assume that neither the driver nor the passenger has a GPS device. The driver is the one behind the wheel, and he (or she) gets lost. As the passenger, do you take the wheel? I sure hope not. As the passenger, you give verbal instructions to the driver. These instructions may include landmarks and directional vocabulary. If the passenger starts by saying, *"Go here," "Go there," "Turn this way," "Go that way,"* then he or she will quickly see how frustrated the driver becomes. By giving clear, verbal instructions with the end goal in one's mind, the passenger is better able to communicate to the driver without taking control of the wheel or overwhelming the driver.

The keys here are in building one's computing vocabulary and collaborating effectively with others. In pair programming, the driver and the navigator take turns operating under the different roles. If they were completing a multi-level program, then the students would switch roles following each level. If they're solving a bigger problem, then they can swap turns every few minutes or after a defined goal is achieved. Pair programming builds rapport and trust, as the students are able to see each other's strengths in problem-solving.

As we introduce pair programming to our students, we also need to show them what the physical expectations are. Often, students will physically take over a device when working in pairs. We need to teach them that working together is not the same as doing it for them.

I had a colleague once who had a floating quote on his screensaver:

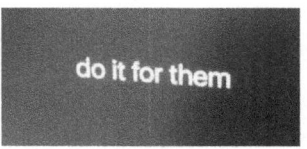

When we convey the message that it's easier to do things for people, then there are no true winners. One student builds on his or her ability while the other student falls further and further behind. There's an old Chinese proverb we often hear in education that exemplifies this more exactly:

Tell me, I will forget.
Show me, I may remember.
Involve me, and I will understand.

By focusing on the practice of pair programming being more than just show-and-tell, we're adding value to the learning experience.
    Sometimes while participating in pair programming, I have students who complain to me that their partners just aren't getting it. I ask them what they've done. I have them show me their process. Then I explain how no two learners will learn in the exact same way. Just as we work in small groups to differentiate instruction in math class, the pair within pair programming must figure out how each partner learns best.

Learning Styles

Knowing your students' learning styles and ensuring that they know their own learning styles will help as they learn through pair programming. The learning styles are as follows:

- Visual
- Auditory
- Kinesthetic
- Solitary
- Verbal
- Social
- Logical[56]

When students are aware of both their own and their partners' learning styles, it gives them a deeper understanding of how both they and their partners learn best.

Visual learners thrive on the use of images and visual depictions to understand concepts. Thus, when their partners work with them, they may find that their best option is to model the computational thinking and problem-solving processes for their partners.

Auditory learners learn best by listening and may prefer instructions to be verbally repeated to fully understand a concept. Their partners need to be aware of this because the auditory learner may ask for information or for an explanation to be repeated not because the student doesn't understand, or is not listening but because he or she needs to hear it over and over again to instill the information into his or her brain.

Kinesthetic learners best understand through tactile experiences. This means that their best approach to learning is one in which they can experience hands-on learning. Working with this type of learner requires a stronger inquiry approach, with the partner asking, "What would happen if you switched these pieces?" Getting these learners to physically experience the programs they build is key to understanding how each unique program works. These learners are also likely to be keen on physical computing. Within physical computing, components have to be manipulated in the physical world to correspond with the code that is created in the virtual world and vice versa.

Solitary learning is likely one of the more difficult learning styles. Solitary learners prefer to learn in isolation from others. Thus, when it comes to pair programming, they are the students who are most likely to pull back from the rest of the herd. However, it is important that these learners are integrated into the classroom learning experience because as they mature into adulthood, they will need to know how to work with others in collaborative working environments.

Verbal learners will need to speak through their learning process. These learners model what we should see in an inquiry-driven learning environment. Speaking through their process with aided questioning allows these learners to verbally diagnose the problems with their programs. Remember my driver's education example? The same context applies here. When speaking the steps of the process, verbal learners are able to understand how to enable their programs to work.

Social learners thrive in group environments. It's important that these learners are contributing and can relate to their partners' learning styles. Social learners can often overtake the learning process, so it is important that they maintain a balance of give-and-take when participating in pair programming. Creating a normative environment around balance will allow these social learners to self-regulate and to let others thrive.

Logical learners can reason, solve problems, and learn using numbers and the analysis of cause-and-effect relationships. These learners thrive in coding as a whole because they can effectively problem solve, digging away at how the program works. When it comes to vocabulary terms, these learners are likely to pick up on the meaning and application of conditionals (which we'll review in more depth in chapter 9) quicker than most other learners.

Conditionals are the logical "*if-then*" statements that state that if one thing happens, then another thing will happen as a result.

Visual learners learn best through modeling. In some cases, students may find that modeling a process on their own devices works best when practicing pair programming on difficult tasks. By modeling, the driver can see the passenger's process. Modeling is a very important practice to use with visual learners, especially as the visual impact that a program has creates a mental imprint that students are able to recall as they advance in their coding journeys.

In pair programming, as well as in many other areas of instruction, consider using an Asian approach when having students help one another. When you need help in several Asian countries, you ask an auntie or an uncle. The term *auntie* refers to how an individual would call out for assistance from a woman. In the United States, we use the term *ma'am* to do this. *Uncle* refers to how an individual would call out for assistance from a man. In the United States, we use the term *sir* to accomplish this. When aunties or uncles help us, they do so with their hands behind their backs, using only their heads and words to provide assistance. This may be through speaking, nodding, or even a combination of the two. By doing this, the auntie or uncle is providing assistance without taking over the wheel—without doing it for the learner.

Using this hands-off method of supporting one another gets students to hone in on their speaking and listening standards[57]:

- Staying on topic (SL.1)
- Asking questions to check for understanding (SL.1)
- Explaining their ideas (SL.1)
- Active listening (SL.3)
- Speaking clearly (SL.6)
- Sharing facts (SL.4)

Creating the correct pairs is of great importance and should focus less on ability and more on the learner type. In education, we're moving away from equality in order to better focus on equity. Equality is treating everyone the same, whereas equity is giving everyone what they need to be successful. To be successful, our more quiet students must be paired with someone who won't steal the show, taking away their self-confidence as a trophy. To successfully pair up your students, look to see what their learner types are instead of focusing on their ability levels. When introducing coding into your curriculum, especially for a student's very first time, this practice of purposeful pairing will ensure that there is equity in both students' voices as they collaboratively approach the problem-solving tasks of coding.

When we group based on ability level instead of on learner type, we risk diminishing one student while boosting the other one. For example, some pairs in our math classes have one high-level student paired with one low-level student. In this high-low pairing, who do you think will have the loudest voice? Who will be the most frustrated student? Who will move further ahead? Who will fall further behind?

Another grouping seen in classes around the world is randomly selecting boys and girls as partners or choosing pairs based on the pull of a stick. When this random grouping occurs, we risk having a high-ability, loud boy paired with a high-ability, quiet girl or vice versa. When this happens, the loud student, regardless of gender, tends to win. However, if we were to flip that pair and put the high-ability, loud boy together with a high-ability, loud girl, then what we see is both equal and equitable. This pairing is equal in the sense that the students are of equal ability levels and, more importantly, learner profile types, and it is equitable in that it provides both individuals with what they need to be successful.

For the sake of gender equity, how you pair students matters. By taking the gender and ability levels out of it and focusing instead on learning styles, you're able to create an environment where every individual is granted the power to discover and use their own brains and their own voices.

Keep in mind that the whole purpose of pair programming is to create equitable pairs to solve problems, not to pit them against each other.

Allow the Student to Become the Expert

Allowing your students to become the experts is all about giving them a chance to shine.

In my work as an educational technology coach, I support teachers in implementing meaningful technology integration into the classroom. Time and time again, a teacher will book me into his or her classroom to teach a tool. Every time this happens, I start the mini lesson with a question:

"Who can teach me how to _____?"

By putting a question back on the learners in the room, we're empowering them to use both their minds *and* their voices to figure out how to solve a problem and to voice the solution in a coherent way that will make sense to the other learners in the room.

In one scenario, the teacher had booked me for an hour-long lesson to teach her students how to use an iPad app called Explain Everything[58] to record their problem-solving process for a math lesson. Explain Everything has a great number of features that would have easily taken me the entire hour to introduce to the students. However, the goal was not to learn the ins and outs of Explain Everything but to use the tool to have students record their problem-solving process for a math lesson. Upon entering the class, I shared the lesson objective with the students and then asked them if they had ever heard of or used the app.

Almost every hand in the class shot up.

If we're not asking our students the most general questions, then we're not allowing them to become the experts in the room. My job as a coach and as an educator is not to do the work for the learners but to guide them through the process of figuring it out for themselves.

From the several hands that shot up, I selected one student to guide me through the problem-solving journey. I want to annotate a document. *How do I do that?* I want to add a slide. *What button do I need to press?* I need to record my voice as I flip through the slides. *How do I do that?*

My job in this process was not to teach the tool but to ask the right questions and to find the experts in the room who would publicly guide me through the problem-solving process. I ran us into a few roadblocks from time to time, and the students were able to come together and help me through the tricky pieces. When I would genuinely get stuck on something, the students were quick to offer up a variety of solutions, many of which worked.

This is how students can become the experts in the room. When we open up our challenges and problems to students for their feedback, we're building on their confidence and showing them that we believe in them. Gone are the days when teachers are the only experts in the room.

Think-Pair-Share

To begin implementing this practice into your instruction, start with a think-pair-share. Think-pair-share gets students to develop bravery by interacting with others and voicing their solutions, even though they may be wrong or half-baked. By being allotted the time to think on their own first, students have an opportunity to work a problem out in their own minds. As they do this, they begin to understand that they don't have to be right on the first thought. No one knows what's going on in his or her mind, and no one knows if they're right or not yet. Once students have a few minutes to think about the problem that you have given them, then it's time for them to pair off with another student.

Pairing allows students to share their solutions with a partner, thereby iterating how they approached the problem. Think of it like pair programming. In pair programming, the whole idea is that two brains are better than one. When students understand this point, then we're able to share more; similar to how they do with their pair programming partners. Pairing students similarly to how you paired them as instructed in the chapter on Pair Programming is important. You don't want students who are going to put each other down. You want two students who are similar in personality and learning style, when possible. Maybe the students are in an after-school club together. Maybe they are neighbors. Maybe they eat lunch together. You've seen them talk to each other. Or they could become friends. These are the students you want to pair together. Purposeful pairing builds culture in the community and can create friends for a lifetime.

One thing to avoid is consistently pairing boys with boys and girls with girls. Remember, the point is not to see who is smarter. The point is to build experience and experts in the class. This can't be done if we're pitting girls against boys, even in something as simple as pairing during our think-pair-share.

The final step in a think-pair-share is sharing.

Sharing gets students to speak up, now with the support of one of their fellow classmates. When you ask a pair to share, pay attention to which student you're directing the question to. Are you always asking the same boys or girls to share? If so, why?

When we pose a challenge to pairs, let's make sure that we're bringing it to both partners in the pair. Sometimes we may need to lay it out for students more directly: "Girls and boys, you're going to pair off now based on your birthdays [or family names, first names, or heights]."

Students pair off accordingly.

"The person in your pair who is the oldest [or whose family names start with the earliest letter of the alphabet] is going to be the reporter who shares your solutions with the whole class at the end of this think-pair-share activity."

Getting all students to participate in think-pair-share with different partners gives them the opportunity to work in a supportive environment where they've tried their solutions with a few classmates, thereby giving them the gradual confidence to share more with the class as a whole, which allows them to speak up as the expert in the room.

In addition, *"think-pair-share"* gets students to practice speaking and listening standards. Throughout the Common Core State Standards (CCSS)[59], the first speaking and listening standard explains that students must engage in collaborative discussions. Students as young as kindergarten and preschool are able to initiate and build on these speaking and listening skills. The expectations for high school students are no different. We're trying to get students to become more collaborative citizens. Gone are the days when computer programmers sit in a dark basement programming code until they fall asleep. The expert is not me, and it's not even you. The expert is us. Together as students, girls and boys alike collaborate to find creative solutions; they are becoming experts in their own right.

In my support of teachers and their students, I often knight students as experts. This knighting happens typically within the first five minutes of any learning experience. Once students can fix something or explain how something works, I immediately knight them as experts. All they have to do is explain what happened, why it did, and how it did. When students can use their words to explain their process without putting a single finger on a device, I knight them as experts. As experts, their job now is to help other students become experts as well. It's wizardry of sorts, one where as educators we demystify the mysterious things, allowing students to have "aha" moments. Once they have their "aha" moments, we promote sharing the wizardry with others so that our learning community can echo that of Harry Potter's.

In teaching coding, many educators, particularly those in elementary school, do not have a degree or any formal background in coding. In a field where we're used to being the experts in the room, it's important to know when we're out of our league. False confidence gets you only so far in this world, and when it comes to breaking down coding problems, we need to realize that it's not our job as educators to be the fixers. We must instead look at ourselves as the facilitators of learning and wear our lead inquirer hats. When you witness most of the class experiencing the same roadblock in a coding activity, find your student experts in the room.

Who knows how to solve the problem?

Who knows what one of the steps is or could be toward reaching the solution?

Call on that student to help explain his or her reasoning to the class. And remember, it's not always going to be a boy who has the right answer.

Studies show that when girls don't volunteer to speak up in class, it's because they fear they will be wrong.[60] This lack of confidence is something that is also seen in a great number of female elementary teachers. When we exhibit a lack of confidence in our ability to perform mathematical computations or to participate in computational thinking, we are exemplifying a standard of being not good enough simply because we can't get comfortable in this uncomfortable space.

No one wants to be embarrassed by providing the wrong solution to a problem, but how do we know if the solution is wrong if we're never giving students the chance to think for themselves?

Culture is defined as a group of people who come together around a common set of values and beliefs.[61] We have a culture in our classrooms. The sharing of these beliefs and values forms trust. Trust allows us to take risks and to feel supported in our efforts, come success or failure. When we ride a bike, we start with the training wheels on. After some time, we develop the courage to take those training wheels off. When we speak in front of a group of our friends, we are exhibiting trust because we know that if we forget our words, then they won't laugh us off the stage.

To build up our students' confidence, especially that which lies within girls, we need to focus more on the process of learning and less on the product. The more we focus on and provide points for sharing, the more likely girls are to step up and become the expert.

Imagine this.

You're sitting in class, and the teacher asks, *"Who knows how to achieve a specific coding goal?"* The teacher offers one try point[62] to the class for every unique attempt someone shares. Then, whenever the students in the class offer a try that works, the class gets a fly point.[63] When all the points are added up, the class has five to ten times as many try points as they do fly points.

The purpose of try and fly points is to make the learning process transparent. Students need to understand that they won't always be able to get the correct answer to a problem on their first try. By recognizing coding as a process rather than as an end product, students can see their growth through a graphing of their failed attempts. They need to recognize that these fails are not failures to learn but rather failures to succeed, which is quite different. When we fail to learn, we fail to grow. When we fail to succeed, we are still learning.

Obtain Base Level Knowledge

When completing lessons before assigning them to the class, the goal is to be at least one step ahead of your students so that if they encounter a problem (that no one else in the class has seen), you can help guide them.

In June 2014, I began working as a consultant for a coding company. The company was still in its start-up phase, creating new ways for students to learn how to code and charging teachers a premium to use the full version of their product. Packing up most of my worldly belongings, I left my school on a Wednesday afternoon to drive from Washington, DC, to Menlo Park, California (the Silicon Valley area), to go to work for this start-up that was only a couple of years out of the gate. My job was to lead and co-lead weekly summer enrichment programs for local students whose parents wanted them to learn how to code.

Having used the company's program with my girls in our after-school program for the last few months, I possessed a wonderful level of (false) confidence, assuming that I actually knew what I was doing. I had learned the ins and outs of how the programs worked, so I just knew that working the summer enrichment program would be super easy.

I was warned.

My new supervisor had told me that the summer enrichment program would be different from what I had been used to, as they were new hybrid programs that the company was testing out. I didn't listen. On the very first day of the enrichment program, several students got stuck at one particular junction. Looking over their shoulders as they struggled in the same spot over and over again, I realized what my supervisor was talking about. These programs were different, all right—they were brand-new! They were the latest minimum viable product (MVP), just good enough to deploy to novice users.

I was the epitome of a deer in headlights. Not knowing what to do, I had to think fast. Thinking on my feet is natural—*when I'm familiar with the problem.* However, when it's a brand-new roadblock, I find that I'm better prepared if I have the time to practice and to break the problem down into smaller pieces. Unfortunately, when you're working with ten students for seven hours a day over the course of an entire week, with no personal break time for you as the facilitator to digest a problem, then it becomes quite stressful to think on the fly.

My only option was to say, *"I don't know"* as one can't effectively have false confidence with students in this scenario, especially teenage ones.

Have you ever been so confident in knowing what would transpire that you didn't bother practicing or studying ahead of time?

As educators, we do this quite a bit. We're familiar with the content or the program, so we assume that a new update provided by the same company will yield change that would only make it easier to navigate, not harder.

Maybe you were introducing a new activity to students that you hadn't actually completed yourself yet. When we take the time to learn what our students will learn before we introduce it to them, we're setting ourselves up for success, allowing fewer opportunities for public pitfalls. Learning a lesson beforehand allows us to have an idea of where our students will get stuck. Once the "ask three before me" strategy has been implemented and exhausted, and you've discovered that there are no experts in your classroom, then it's time to begin adulting and step up to the plate to help guide the whole class in working through this roadblock.

As a guide, your job is to be the lead inquirer, directing students through a line of strategic questioning that will steer them to the solution. By modeling what strategic questioning looks like, students are able to see this form of questioning as something they can add to their own learning toolkits when solving problems.[64] Strong questioning skills allow students to participate in sense-making, which is the number-one skill for the future workforce.[65] Remember, it is not our job as educators to give the answer away or to do the work for our students. By being better prepared to lend support when all the other attempts and practices have been implemented, we are better prepared to effectively support our learners as they encounter these roadblocks. Having the insight into where these roadblocks will occur also enables the teacher to support students in becoming knowledge constructors.[66]

The ISTE Student Standard: Knowledge Constructor 3D says "students build knowledge by actively exploring real-world issues and problems, developing ideas and theories and pursuing answers and solutions."[67] If we are to help students become knowledge constructors, then at the very least we should know what they will be constructing knowledge about, particularly if they were working on a subscribed program where there is only one solution.

Remember, our job as educators is to be the facilitator of learning—the lead inquirer. If we don't know the content, then how can we possibly know which question to lead with?

There's a thin line between bravery and stupidity.

To build both our own confidence and the confidence of our learners, we must prepare by at least reviewing the material that our students will begin learning before they come face-to-face with it.

The new ISTE Standards for Educators identify a set of responsibilities for us to adopt regarding the use of technology in the learning environment. One of the key standards for educators is to be a facilitator. In ISTE Educator Standard 6, educators "facilitate learning with technology to support the achievement of ISTE Student Standards." More specifically, educators are charged with the following:

6A Fostering a culture in which students take ownership of their learning goals and outcomes in both independent and group settings

6B Managing the use of technology and student learning strategies in digital platforms, virtual environments, hands-on makerspaces, or in the field

6C Creating learning opportunities that challenge students to use a design process and computational thinking to innovate and solve problems

6D Modeling and nurturing creativity and creative expression to communicate ideas, knowledge, or connections[68]

Of these standards, 6C and 6D relate the most to why we should be completing lessons before we assign them to the class. Fellow educator Marc Seigel says that he never asks his students to do something that he wouldn't do himself.[69] For one lesson, he had assigned his students with the task of designing a model of a building using a virtual AutoCAD-type of sketching tool. He completed the assignment before he gave it to the class, creating a model of his own house. Doing this provided Marc with the background knowledge necessary to aid students if they got stuck with the project. He may not have used every piece of the program to develop the design, but he had created a wonderful replica of his actual house.

Students knew that they could trust Marc as a pseudo expert on the platform because they *saw* what he was able to create. We call this strategy *"show what you know"*. When we put our work, both our successes and our failed attempts, on display, then it in turn creates a learning balance within our ecosystem. Our students can identify with us as fellow learners because we are facilitating the learning with technology for them to transparently see.

Another fellow educator who works with students in understanding computer science is Rafranz Davis.[70] Rafranz spends time experimenting with new technologies that she then introduces to the students she works with. She is a creator. "For me, it's about knowing what I'm talking about and having the knowledge to not just challenge and question but to truly mentor," says Davis. She shares on social media "because hopefully it'll challenge educators to tinker and make. I seek understanding from subject expert teachers in science and CTE as well as industry experts in the field. When teaching students, learning alongside them is perfectly OK, but you have to possess some base level knowledge which absolutely includes having had built something yourself."

The objective in completing a lesson before assigning it is to understand how a program works. You don't need full-on notes or cheat sheets to make copies of for the students who will struggle. You just need an iterative mindset and the time to try an activity out before assigning it to students. This will ensure that students are able to see that you are a learner, just like them. They will respect you not for what you know but for your preparedness and your willingness to try.

In order to foster this culture of sharing, there must be some base trust. When we seek medical advice, we're likely to trust the advice of someone with "Dr." before his or her name. Though we sometimes consult WebMD more often than we go to a professional, when we do visit the doctor, we expect that person to know what he or she is doing, especially when that individual is a specialist of some sort. We expect this because we know (or rightfully assume) that they have gone to college. Their degrees are hung proudly on the walls behind their desks as symbols of what they've accomplished. We trust them when we see this. Seeing this reaffirms our belief that they have completed their required learning before our appointment.

With a doctor, there is a degree requirement. With teaching or learning coding (at the time of this publication), there is not. The absence of a degree or certification doesn't mean that we get a pass; if anything, it means that we need to transparently prove ourselves a bit more than our degreed counterparts. The exciting thing about teaching coding is that this ability to prove ourselves is as simple as showing students what we've been able to create. At the very least, it serves as a benchmark for them to reach and often even surpass.

One way to begin sharing is by publicly presenting your learning journey with fellow educators on social media. This creates transparency and identifies you as a learner. This also gives you a safe space to iterate in before you interact with your students in their lesson attempts. ISTE Educator Standard: Collaborator 4B states that "educators collaborate and co-learn with students to discover and use new digital resources and diagnose and troubleshoot technology issues."[71] In coming prepared to co-learn with students, we are able to model what an iterative and innovative learner looks like, giving students the confidence needed to persevere on their problem-solving journeys.

There's this confidence that we have as humans when we are genuinely prepared. When girls see this, they admire it. It gives them an example to look up to, to aspire to be like. Being prepared is not about an outward look but about an internal preparation. When girls see this in their female educators, they are able to see a model of glowing confidence based on background knowledge and ability, not physical looks.

Working in a school where a large percentage of the IT support staff are women, my heart was overjoyed when one of my grade-five students asked me how one of our IT women became so smart. The student had brought in a personal computer that she was having some issues with, and within just a few minutes of taking it over to our IT department, the issues were resolved. The student was genuinely impressed and amazed. When she inquired through me to find out how the IT woman knew how to fix her computer, I pushed her to ask the IT woman directly. She and her friends did. They started by thanking her, complimenting her efficiency, and then asking her how she learned how to fix computers.

Getting this perspective and hearing this woman's story of her own knowledge acquisition opened the young girls' eyes to the possibilities they might be interested in pursuing one day. By showing up prepared, having at least practiced a lesson or skill first, we are able to exemplify the empowered learner role that we want our students to fulfill in their own rights.

Modeling problem-solving procedures with a prepared background enables girls to see that when the right pieces come together, and with the right steps put in place, anything can be achieved. By thinking out loud, one can navigate through a problem, modeling what that process looks like.

Depending on the type of coding that your students are learning, this practice can be one of the most expensive practices in terms of time. Learning how to code is not something where success is achieved overnight. Thus, if you are truly to prepare for your class, then completing lessons ahead of time is something that requires more than a night's worth of preparation. Some students may progress in the coding very swiftly; others may be more deliberate in their practice, aiming for perfection on the first try, and not even run their programs to test them until they've reached their version of perfection.

For the purpose of obtaining base level knowledge, it is essential to restate the importance of iteration in learning coding. Nothing happens overnight. Small light bursts may occur throughout the synapses of one's brain, but the big eureka moment is one that is harder to achieve in an environment of immediate gratification.

Reflecting and Learning Keywords

This chapter focuses on the pause-and-reflect aspect of learning how to code, as well as the importance of learning keywords. We begin by weaving in where keywords fit within the learning process for coding.

Learning Keywords

One of the biggest reflection points here relates to learning a coding vocabulary. By learning the definitions of words such as *loop*, *conditional*, *sprite*, and *restitution*, you're better able to explain the meaning of these words to students.

My very first week of working with a coding company several summers ago, I had arrived on Sunday afternoon, after spending four days driving cross-country on a solo road trip, with very little time to actually practice the programs prior to the first day of camp. I was able to wing it the first day; however, when day two came around, I hit a major roadblock. As the students were working on their activities, I was asked a question about the meaning of a word. The word was *restitution*. More accurately, the term was the *coefficient of restitution*. I stumbled. I asked for a description of how the student was trying to use the block. The student wanted to know what the block did and was unsure of how to use the block. I redirected the student to do some more independent inquiry, as I went to the other side of the room, retrieving my phone to stealthily Google the right answer.

Google was of no help.

The commonly known definition for restitution is the restoration of something lost or stolen to its proper owner. This definition was not the answer I was looking for.

Luckily, I wasn't the only adult in the room. Upon asking my counterpart for support, he explained to me and the whole class that the restitution of an object is actually the bounciness of an object. The coefficient of restitution is a physics term that is described as a number, which indicates how much kinetic energy (energy of motion) remains after a collision of two objects. If the coefficient of restitution is high (close to 1.00), then it means that very little kinetic energy was lost during the collision.

Why would students need to know about restitution? you ask. This student's program involved making a cannon game, which required the cannonballs to bounce.

Vocabulary is everything. In reading, if students get stuck on a word, then we guide them toward using context clues to construct meaning. In coding, students are exposed to a whole new set of vocabulary words they've likely never used before or that may have a different meaning in a different context. We often find homonyms in coding programs. In a noncoding context, the word may mean one thing, while in the coding context it means something different altogether. Context helps when we're teaching students the definitions of words.

Standard 4 of the CCSS language standards is all about determining the meaning of words, including multiple-meaning words. Thus, incorporating vocabulary into the teaching of coding allows students' development of knowledge, and it allows their ability to implement language skills into their understanding of coding to grow.

As you can see from this list of the CCSS, the ability to understand multiple-meaning words is one that links across grade levels:

Table 9.1: Common Core State Standard Language Standard 4[72]

L.K.4	Determine or clarify the meaning of unknown and multiple-meaning words and phrases based on kindergarten reading and content.
L.1.4	Determine or clarify the meaning of unknown and multiple-meaning words and phrases based on grade 1 reading and content, choosing flexibly from an array of strategies.
L.2.4	Determine or clarify the meaning of unknown and multiple-meaning words and phrases based on grade 2 reading and content, choosing flexibly from an array of strategies.
L.3.4	Determine or clarify the meaning of unknown and multiple-meaning words and phrases based on grade 3 reading and content, choosing flexibly from a range of strategies.
L.4.4	Determine or clarify the meaning of unknown and multiple-meaning words and phrases based on grade 4 reading and content, choosing flexibly from a range of strategies.
L.5.4	Determine or clarify the meaning of unknown and multiple-meaning words and phrases based on grade 5 reading and content, choosing flexibly from a range of strategies.

Table 9.1: Common Core State Standard Language Standard 4 cont'd

L.6.4	Determine or clarify the meaning of unknown and multiple-meaning words and phrases based on grade 6 reading and content, choosing flexibly from a range of strategies.
L.7.4	Determine or clarify the meaning of unknown and multiple-meaning words and phrases based on grade 7 reading and content, choosing flexibly from a range of strategies.
L.8.4	Determine or clarify the meaning of unknown and multiple-meaning words and phrases based on grade 8 reading and content, choosing flexibly from a range of strategies.
L.9–10.4	Determine or clarify the meaning of unknown and multiple-meaning words and phrases based on grades 9–10 reading and content, choosing flexibly from a range of strategies.
L.11–12.4	Determine or clarify the meaning of unknown and multiple-meaning words and phrases based on grades 11–12 reading and content, choosing flexibly from a range of strategies.

Standard 4 focuses on the clarification of unknown and multiple-meaning words. By introducing vocabulary words in a mini lesson prior to students experiencing coding activities, we can essentially teach them the strategies for differentiating between word meanings and later assess them on their ability to use the correct word in the correct context for their coding activities.

When we create power standards for reading and writing, an area that is frequently excluded is that of language. By making language learning a priority and infusing it into coding learning opportunities, we can accomplish more cross-curricular learning.

To prepare students for these vocabulary roadblocks, consider creating a word bank of all the terms that students may encounter in their programs. This word bank is something where the contents are introduced to students as they are encountered in the program. Teaching and decoding the meaning of words in a just-in-time fashion allows students to build their understanding of words in that moment, applying their meaning immediately. If, on the other hand, you want to see the lightbulbs go off, then introduce a few of the keywords (or all of them) at the beginning of the lesson. This will cause students to call on their prior knowledge throughout the course of the lesson.

The nice thing about coding is that many of the software and programs already have these vocabulary banks built into their platforms. It is just a matter of us knowing what these words are and where to find them in case students get stuck on the function or meaning of a block or a piece of code.

The following sections detail some of the most common vocabulary terms found in coding programs and how one might explain the definition to students.

Conditionals

Within coding activities, there are things called conditionals. A conditional is an "if this, then that" statement. When introducing students to the concept of a conditional, we can use real-world examples to better facilitate the "aha" moments in the classroom. The following are a few examples:

If you don't finish your dinner, then you won't get dessert.

If you jump up, then you will fall down.

If you tie your shoes, then you won't trip over your shoelaces.

These are all real-life examples that students can relate to. When introducing the concept, start with these examples or a few of your own that directly relate to the learners in your community. Once the lightbulbs begin going off, have students expound on the concept, creating their own conditional statements related to real-life situations. Getting students to think out loud and work through the process of these logic-based conditionals aids in their problem-solving ability as they approach coding. When they use a conditional in their programs, they are better able to understand that the action they choose will have a reaction.

Loops

What happens when you Hula-Hoop? The Hula-Hoop goes round and round and round. This is the same action of a loop. A loop allows a specific piece of the program it contains to repeat. Some loops will allow a program to repeat forever. Some will allow the program to repeat a specific number of times. Some loops will even allow the program to repeat until a specific action occurs or is encountered.

The piece that students often neglect here is defining where the loop will occur and what it will contain. By just adding the word *repeat*, it's like talking to a roomful of people and asking, "What's your name?" when you only wanted the name of one person. When you ask the room, "What's your name?" then everyone may answer, and they'll all answer something different. Instead, identifying the woman in the blue sweater and asking her, "What's your name?" would yield a response from only the woman in the blue sweater.

Specificity in coding is a key detail that is often overlooked. If we're not specifying what we're looking for, then we're likely to get a response that does not fit our intended request. Our intentions were not clear to begin with, so how could the program know what we were hoping to achieve? Programs are smart, but they're only as smart as the programmer. If we haven't told the program to read our minds, then we must ensure that the directions we prescribe are relevant to the specific outcome we hope to achieve.

Variables

Variables are numbers or colors. In coding, a variable often represents the quantity of times that an action will occur. These variables are consistently used in conjunction with loops, as having a loop by itself with no variable implies that the action will repeat indefinitely (forever) or until something prevents it from moving any further.

Actions

Actions are things that will occur. The character will move ten pixels forward. The background will change when a button is pressed. The points will increase as two objects collide. The actions are the pieces of a program that enable it to actually *do* something. However, an action cannot occur if it is not assigned to anything. Imagine that you want a character to move forward. If you didn't start by defining what the character was, then you can't very well tell it what to do. As students first start out on their coding journeys, they often forget the first piece of the program. They forget to define what they're controlling. The process should go as follows:

1. Define the object to be controlled.
2. Control the defined object.

Pause and Reflect

To better recall the meaning of vocabulary words and their implications within coding activities, consider providing your learners with an opportunity to pause and reflect. This could occur at the end of a lesson or activity, or it could occur at the end of a project creation. By regularly reflecting on their coding journeys, as well as on their progress and setbacks, students are better able to capture and share their learning. In going back to read these posts and reflections, students can continuously call on their previous experiences to ensure that they don't make the same mistakes over and over again. Provide students with the following questions to respond to in their reflection posts:

1. What were the peaks?
2. What were the pits?
3. What is my plan or goal for next time?

By getting students to pause and reflect on their learning, they are utilizing CCSS Writing Standard 8, which is all about recalling information from experiences. Although this standard focuses on recall of information in kindergarten through grade five, it grows into "gathering relevant information from multiple print and digital resources" for middle school and high school. This standard growth allows students to think beyond their experiences and to begin incorporating the *how* into their explanations of what worked and what didn't. The prompts for these middle school and high school pause-and-reflect moments can support students' understanding of computer science by explaining how it all works.

Standard 8 of the CCSS writing standards evolves in the following way:

Table 9.2: Common Core State Standard Writing Standard 8[73]

W.K.8	With guidance and support from adults, recall information from experiences or gather information from provided sources to answer a question.
W.1.8	With guidance and support from adults, recall information from experiences or gather information from provided sources to answer a question.
W.2.8	Recall information from experiences or gather information from provided sources to answer a question.
W.3.8	Recall information from experiences or gather information from print and digital sources; take brief notes on sources and sort evidence into provided categories.

Table 9.2: Common Core State Standard Writing Standard 8 cont'd

W.4.8	Recall relevant information from experiences or gather relevant information from print and digital sources; take notes and categorize information and provide a list of sources.
W.5.8	Recall relevant information from experiences or gather relevant information from print and digital sources; summarize or paraphrase information in notes and finished work and provide a list of sources.
W.6.8	Gather relevant information from multiple print and digital sources, assess the credibility of each source, and quote or paraphrase the data and conclusions of others while avoiding plagiarism and providing basic bibliographic information for sources.
W.7.8	Gather relevant information from multiple print and digital sources, using search terms effectively; assess the credibility and accuracy of each source; and quote or paraphrase the data and conclusions of others while avoiding plagiarism and following a standard format for citation.
W.8.8	Gather relevant information from multiple print and digital sources, using search terms effectively; assess the credibility and accuracy of each source; and quote or paraphrase the data and conclusions of others while avoiding plagiarism and following a standard format for citation.
W.9–10.8	Gather relevant information from multiple authoritative print and digital sources, using advanced searches effectively; assess the usefulness of each source in answering the research question; integrate information into the text selectively to maintain the flow of ideas, avoiding plagiarism and following a standard format for citation.

Table 9.2: Common Core State Standard Writing Standard 8 cont'd

W.11–12.8	Gather relevant information from multiple authoritative print and digital sources, using advanced searches effectively; assess the strengths and limitations of each source in terms of the task, purpose, and audience; integrate information into the text selectively to maintain the flow of ideas, avoiding plagiarism and overreliance on any one source and following a standard format for citation.

When working with middle school and high school students, provide them with the following questions to respond to in their reflection posts:

1. How did you get your program to _____?

2. Why does or doesn't your program work?

3. Providing examples of resources that you have used or will use, what will you do next time?

Incorporating key words and providing students with the time and opportunity to pause and reflect gives them an equitable opportunity for time to understand how their programs work or don't work. It is this notion of time that we tend to neglect in the learning process. By giving students time to digest a problem, as well as the keywords needed to decipher meaning, we are giving them a chance to succeed in the acquisition of their own knowledge in the area of coding.

Remember, success in the world's first-ever flight did not happen overnight. Thus, when we give our students a chance to build programs from the ground up, we should allow them ample time to digest, learn, and reflect along the way.

Part 3

Initiatives for Empowering Girls

This section focuses on some of the tried-and-true ways of increasing the number of girls who take on coding courses and clubs in their academic careers. These approaches come from private, public, international, and single-gender school settings.

From Blogging Club to Coding Club

How you market these coding clubs to your students means everything. When we start a club, we often take the stance that if students don't sign up, then it means they're not interested. If we live with this assumption, then no one wins, as we'll continue to have imbalanced coding clubs, where girls fail to see any opportunity for entry.

When I first began teaching girls to code, I was at an all-girls public charter school. The school was only three years old when I began working there, so testing out new programs and initiatives was easy to do, as the school was already in a state of constant change, making pivots toward perfection. As the technology teacher, during my first year, I got to know the girls pretty well. We had preschool through grade five that year, and I found that the fourth and fifth graders needed something more than the day-to-day academic aspect of school life.

I should explain.

This all-girls school was located in the poorest ward of a major city, with an unemployment rate of 30 percent. When unemployment rates are that high, it's an indication that the community is in dire need of some type of change or reform. The school's founder created the school with the needs of the community in mind. With the risk of getting into drugs, gangs, or worse, the school community knew we had to offer these girls some type of positive outlet.

During my second year at the school, I was able to write a proposal and job description that would transition me from the school's technology teacher to the education technology coordinator, the first the school had ever had on both counts (*one day I'll coauthor a book on how this professional advancement came about*). Starting with a daily news program run by girls as young as preschool, I was able to see many of them transform from at-risk youth into empowered young women who were allowed to have a voice in the messages that the other girls in their learning community were hearing. We had used the computer lab (that was predominantly used for standardized state testing) and a large green cloth to function as the green screen background with little more than an iPad and a makeshift stand to create the newscast that we would prerecord the afternoon before it was to be shared with the whole school via morning announcements. This student-led newscast was a great start, but I wanted to do more.

In an effort to provide opportunities for these girls that would hopefully ensure that they didn't follow the path of drugs, gangs, and jail (as many of their friends and families had been a part of), I offered an after-school blogging club. Writing has always been therapeutic for me, so I thought I'd have the girls give it a try. Because they needed writing practice for the upcoming state test, I figured this blogging club could provide them with the practice they needed to succeed while also giving them a voice, a creative outlet. We chose new topics each week. Sometimes we focused on hopes and dreams, and other times we wrote in response to something that had happened in our community. After a few months of the blogging club, I noticed my girls' enthusiasm waning. Maybe we had run out of topics, maybe I was out of inspiration, or maybe the timing had just been wrong. I knew that I wanted something that would challenge my girls and their ability to think critically and analytically, and this blogging club simply wasn't cutting it any longer.

Around this same time, Code.org launched the Hour of Code week. During the first week in December 2013, classes throughout the school partook in the free coding activities that were hosted on HourofCode.com. I excitedly went from class to class, launching students and teachers on their journeys to learn how to code. In those very basic activities that were offered during Code.org's early days, I began to make connections to the curriculum that would greatly amplify students' understanding of math concepts while also learning how to program, how to iterate, and how to practice computational thinking. There is a section of Code.org's programs (that still exists as of the publication date of this book) where coding activities integrate with mathematical concepts, such as angle degrees and measurement.

I remember being so excited to see so many of our classes participate in the Hour of Code week that year. In particular, I was quite impressed by the gains of the girls who received learning support. Taking this elation, I ran with it!

That spring we turned our blogging club into a coding club. Using Tynker, a tool that I had learned about during the Hour of Code week, I had the girls complete challenges and advance through the courses to acquire the skills to create anything they set their minds to. The girls were in the zone, and this is when I noticed something quite peculiar but that really makes sense when you pause to think about it. The girls who were academically low were the girls who were able to iterate and understand the computing concepts faster than the girls who were academically high.

One girl encountered a part of her program where she wanted her character to turn around. With this program using degrees as a measurement of rotation, we had to review the concept of a degree. I began the mini lesson, which lasted all of five minutes, by drawing a picture of a circle on the board. I explained to this young third-grader that she should imagine she is in the true center point of the circle facing true north, also known as zero degrees. I gave her the fact that a circle is made up of 360 degrees. The road we were heading down began to click for the girl.

Figure 10.1: Drawing a circle to understand degrees

I asked, "If this bottom point cuts the circle in half, then what is the degree measurement of each part?"

Doing the math calculation on the board, she said, "180 degrees."

"Very good," I said.

"Now, if we cut this half of the circle in half, then what would the degree measurement be?" I asked.

Conducting the mathematical calculation on the board once again, the young girl said, "90 degrees."

"You're right!" I said.

Following this brief interactive inquiry into a topic, the girl was not only able to control the character in her program the way she wanted to; she was also able to teach this concept to the other girls in the coding club.

In this coding club setting, I conducted an action research study, examining the learning progressions of girls in the area of mathematical and reading concepts as they developed their coding acumen. On February 11, 2014, I gave the girls a survey that centered on a variety of reading and mathematical concepts that they may or may not have learned by this time. The survey consisted of sixteen questions that were linked to the CCSS. By the end of our coding club that spring, I gave the girls the same survey again. Having been about two months since we began coding, several of the girls improved their scores very quickly. Even though they were in younger grades, they still were able to learn about more advanced mathematical skills that they hadn't yet been exposed to in their own math classes. Several were able to build their skills while also learning how to fail fast and learn more from the process than from their products. This lesson on failing is an urgent need, as failing is something that all humans do at some point.

The questions on the survey were as follows:

1. Solve.
   $63 - 19 =$

2. Solve for X.
   $43 - X =$

3. What set of numbers completes the following sequence?
   9, 18, 27

4. Solve.
   (18 + 6) − 2 =

5. Write a related subtraction fact for 14 − 2 = 12.

6. You have $28.75. You buy a guitar for $19.98. How much change will you get back?

7. Which word is the subject of the following sentence?
   "Her turtle ate eighteen fish."

8. Which sentence is correct?
   "Becky went to the Nationals' baseball game with her brother, Tom."
   "Becky went to the nationals' Baseball Game with her brother, tom."
   "Becky went to the Nationals' Baseball Game with her brother Tom."

9. What does *mistreat* mean?

10. Which word is the action verb?
    "The sun shines so bright at lunchtime."

11. Is the sentence in the past, present, or future tense?
    "Mya is trying to tie her shoe."

12. Which sentence is correct?
    "Jane and Judy just finished watching *SpongeBob SquarePants* on Nickelodeon."
    "Jane and judy just finished watching spongebob squarepants on nickelodeon."
    "Jane and Judy just finished watching spongebob squarepants on Nickelodeon."

13. What does *limitless* mean?

14. Complete the sentence with the correct helping verb(s).
    "David couldn't hear you because he _____ playing his music too loud."

15. Which verb best completes the sentence?
    "There is no snow on the ground, so we _____ go to school today."

16. What does *preorder* mean?

Their scores (out of sixteen total points) were as follows:

Table 10.1: Survey results from CCSS-aligned assessment on coding

	First Survey (February 2014)	Second Survey (May 2014)
Student A (Gr 5)	13	13
Student B (Gr 3)	8	9
Student C (Gr 5)	16	15
Student D (Gr 5)	8	13
Student E (Gr 5)	9	12
Student F (Gr 3)	15	14
Student G (Gr 4)	2	3
Student H (Gr 4)	5	6
Student I (Gr 4)	9	9
Student J (Gr 5)	10	13
Student K (Gr 4)	8	6

Of the eleven students who participated in this study, you can see how more than half of them (six) were able to improve their survey scores after only two months of learning how to code for the first time. Two students maintained their scores from the first to the second survey, and three students regressed by one or two points in between each survey.

In assessing the girls on the language-based skills, I was able to relate their understanding in a connected way to the syntax of scripted coding languages as well as the logic in block-based coding languages. When I posed questions to the girls on mathematical skills, I was homing in on their understanding of the logic of coding.

When we first teach students how to program, regardless of their age levels, it's important to start with the logic because this area of computational thinking will allow students to dissect problems and generate solutions. When students advance into the syntax, they're moving away from the big idea and getting more granular.

The girls were making such large gains in our after-school club that I was able to convince their teachers to allow them to continue with their coding practice during the school day. The teachers immediately saw an increase in engagement from the girls who were in the coding club, as they were now motivated to finish their classwork so that they could commit time to an activity that provided them with both joy and challenge. Little did they know that the concepts they were learning through coding were actually benefiting them in their future math classes. In addition, the way in which they were able to constantly iterate was a skill that would get them far in life.

Made with Code

When Google launched MadewithCode.com[74] in the summer of 2014, I was beyond excited. Finally, an inspirational tool that would get our young, elementary school-level girls interested in learning how to code by allowing them to see how real, modern women have been able to successfully mix coding with one of their other passions.

This was a move in the right direction, especially after Google published its employment report for the whole world to see in May 2014. Although the release is one that many would think to be a jaw-dropping action, the real big moment was in scrolling down the report to see the numbers.

Seventy percent of all Google jobs around the globe went to men, with a mere 30 percent going to women.[75]

Then, when you look at the actual technical jobs, the ones that involve computing to some degree, the percentage of men taking those jobs goes up to 83 percent, with women holding a mere 17 percent.

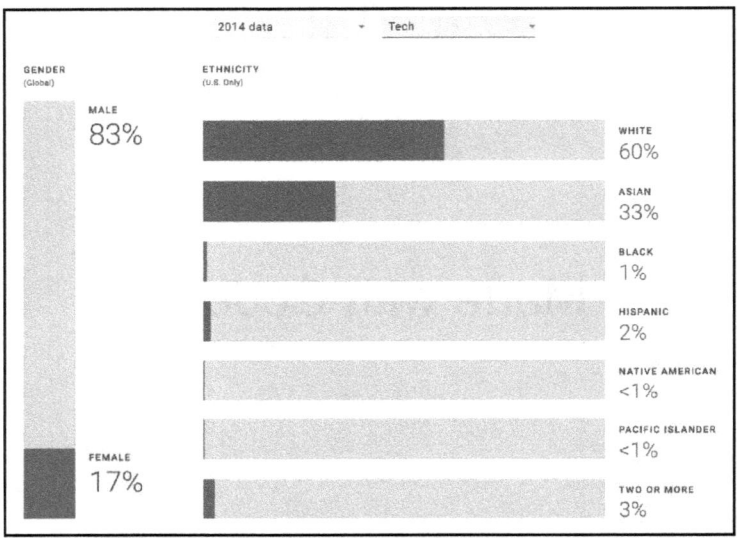

Figure 11.1: Google's 2014 Tech Employment numbers

When we peel back the onion to look one layer deeper, we find that men hold 79 percent of leadership roles, with only 21 percent going to women.

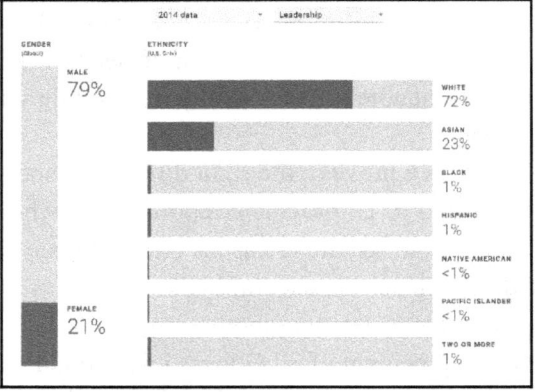

Figure 11.2: Google's 2014 Leadership Employment numbers

The numbers don't lie. Companies considered to be our biggest tech giants like Google, along with many others, are well aware that there's a real problem in regard to the gender gap in the computing world.

There is also racial inequity.

With 60 percent of employees in tech being white, 33 percent being Asian, 1 percent being Black, 2 percent Hispanic, and 3 percent of two or more races, one can easily see where the gap is. But is this a question of inequity or one of inequality?

As a biracial woman working within a white male–dominated industry, I can tell you that several of the issues that arise are ones that center on both equity and equality. I have seen, time after time, white men advanced into positions of leadership ahead of similarly-skilled women simply because they are white men, one of the "good ole boys."

Google's move to publicly share its employment report was brave and bold, allowing us to better understand the necessity of getting girls interested in coding. It should also be of no surprise that Google immediately dropped a whopping $50 million investment into MadewithCode.com as a way to inspire young girls to pursue the male-dominated field of computer science.[76] Although the investment has yet (as of the date of this publication) to offset the overall employment numbers, the important thing to note is that through this program, girls can now have real-life women and fellow girls to aspire to be like in a way that mixes their passions with coding.

Shortly after MadewithCode.com launched, I began working at a small, rural, K–8 public school. The community's main economies were farming and manufacturing. My role in this environment focused on instructional technology coaching. Starting first with launching a campus-wide Chromebook initiative, I opted to let the dust settle before getting the teachers on board with coding integration in their classrooms.

In the spring of that school year, I planned a girls' coding party on a Saturday afternoon. Girls could invite their moms to participate in this event, but it was essentially an activity that allowed girls to bond and build a sisterhood of support while they iterated through a series of creative coding activities.

MadewithCode.com offers a start-up guide for hosting events. We followed this guide to get girls to spend a Saturday at school, where they began to learn about an area of study in which they might decide to find or create future employment opportunities.

The Hour of Code—
A Family Night

On December 9, 2013, Code.org launched the first-ever Hour of Code week worldwide. With a goal of getting students around the world to try out one hour of code, this initiative has taken off since its inception.

The second annual Hour of Code was coming up, and I wanted to host an event to get our parent community involved.

On December 13, 2014, I coordinated an Hour of Code family event. Communications went home to our students' families, informing them of this amazing opportunity to get a taste of learning how to code *with* their students for an hour. We didn't collect RSVPs, so there was no way to know how many families would show up. We had Chromebooks set up with different coding activities. The students who had already been practicing coding in their classes were able to have an audience of beta testers to try out their games, giving them constructive feedback on how they might be able to improve their programs. With support from the administrative team, we were able to have pizza delivered and fully paid for by the school.

As families slowly began to trickle in, my public relations background switched on. This night was all about student-empowered learning, giving students an opportunity to iterate without penalty and allowing both parents and children to see and experience "aha" moments in a rapid turnaround. My role was merely to provide suggestions about where parents and their students could begin and to be on standby to aid in the logistics, provide problem-solving strategies through inquiry, and tech support as needed.

We were in a very small town, so getting the local newspaper to come out and do a brief, positive story on this great event was pretty easy. There's always a bit of fear when you invite the press to something that has just launched, particularly when you're unsure as to what your exact attendance numbers might be. But as they say, "Nothing ventured, nothing gained."

When you reach out to those various news outlets, and you're unsure of what attendance will look like, give a range, and use words like *expecting* more often than you use the word *hope*. *Expecting* sets the standard, something that has a high probability of happening, whereas the word *hope* paints a picture of uncertainty, like the inner wanderings of a daydreamer. With PR know-how, I reached out to every outlet I could. In the end, we got coverage from two of the dozen or so sources I contacted. We were also contacted by our local congressman and were able to have him be our guest speaker at the event.

Congressman Bill Foster[77] spoke to our audience of about sixty people toward the beginning of the event. He interacted with our students and their families as they dove into this coding event. Being at the event, he was able to see the iterative impact that learning how to code had on the students. With his background in computer science, it's no wonder that he would be drawn to such an event.

The key in most everything is to know your audience. As I write this book, there are others being published on girls in coding. Those books have a prescribed audience of young girls and their parents, whereas this book is geared toward the educators and school leaders who are aiming to provide a more equitable learning environment, bridging the gender gap.

Having the congressman be the featured speaker at our Hour of Code family event did a lot of good for our school district. The press did its job, and we were able to get a bright light of recognition cast on the school district.

Evolution from Co-ed to Girls Coding Club

In February 2016, while working in an international school, I began an after-school club called the Programming Pioneers Club. I knew I wanted to advocate for the girls; however, I wanted to first see what would happen if I opened up the club to everyone, both boys and girls. Call it a social experiment. Here's what happened.

Twenty-four boys and one girl signed up for that first season of Programming Pioneers Club.

Then, when I received two older students to help me out, I was assigned two male students from the high school. I didn't fully realize how much my heart was breaking—I only felt how hard it was aching. After four weeks of leading this club, I watched the girl grow in her abilities as the boys goofed off and spent most of their time off task. During the fourth week, I noticed that something was wrong. The sole girl wouldn't answer the questions I asked the group. She began hiding at a faraway table, and no one could comfort her. It was a very sad sight to see of this one young girl who was barely eight years old, being outcasted by the boys.

Taking a seat at her table, I asked her what was wrong. She wouldn't tell me at first, so I stayed nearby, patiently giving her the space to open up as much or as little as she wanted to. This girl was strong not only in her computing abilities but also in her abilities to handle the mean words that the boys would say to her. They were telling her that she was stupid; that she didn't know how to code, and that she was ugly. When she shared this with me, a piece of my heart broke. I knew it would be a social experiment to open this club to boys and girls, but I had no idea that boys as young as seven to ten years old would be such big bullies to a girl who was barely eight.

Remember reading in chapter 1 about what had happened regarding that Google memo from the now ex-Googler? That young girl's experience reminds me of the words the writer used in his memo. The boys in my club were bullying the girl, not because she didn't know what she was doing (because she knew her stuff) but because she was a girl who knew more than they did. This behavior was *not* OK with me. I had been having the young girl help the boys who clearly needed it, and the boys were showing their thanks with mean words.

I decided to change things up a little bit. For the last four weeks of our club, I let the well-behaved students work on their coding programs first, having the bullies wait one additional collective minute for every disruption, as their behavior was so negative. This small adjustment was able to change the way the boys behaved in the club and how they interacted with the girl. All the boys weren't bad, so we just had to figure out how to strain out the ones who had a positive impact on the group from the ones who were displaying a negative impact.

After completing this first cohort of the Programming Pioneers Club, I decided to kill it off altogether. Boys already had a leg up because of their gender, and they even had their own gender-specific, Boys Robotics Club.

The next term, I began a brand-new club, a Girls Coding Club. We started with a humble eight girls during that first season and maintained full rosters of twenty to twenty-four girls in the club every season since. Their behavior is not only better than that of the boys', but there is also virtually no bullying whatsoever. The girls support one another naturally, as a sisterhood would. Even with the girls being in different grades (grades three through five), no one has been an island unto herself. They have quickly learned how to ask one another for help. When they get stuck, they don't cry. Instead, they get support from another girl in the room. Twenty-four girls, many starting off as strangers (even within the same grade), have been able to communicate, collaborate, think critically, and create with one another in such a beautiful symphony that they should truly be a model of how we all work together.

Starting the coding club with inquiry-based learning around computational thinking, the girls have been able to successfully fail. To fail successfully, you must fail fast and then get back up and brush yourself off for another attempt, where you may possibly fail again. These girls understand that.

In addition, fostering an environment that moves away from perfection and into the messiness of reality allows the girls to gain more comfort in the ambiguous nature of coding. This environment also provides them with a sense of community that they can rely on as they matriculate into middle school, where the number of girls in coding courses tends to fall off. By creating a strong foundation in a supportive learning community in their early years, girls are exponentially more likely to pursue these STEM-based areas in their middle school programs and beyond.

Technovation Challenge

The Technovation Challenge[78] is an amazing opportunity that provides girls ages 10 to 18 from all over the world the opportunity to come together to solve one of the world's problems. This empowering initiative gets girls to learn how to code with a purpose. Often, when we get students into coding, it starts as a Friday fun-time activity, or maybe it looks more like an enrichment activity. If we're always framing the learning of coding as a conditional "*if this, then that*," then we're not getting down to the true purpose of this learning; we're not defining the *why*.

With the introduction of the Technovation Challenge, girls now have an opportunity to compete in a purpose-based coding challenge that centers on the category of their choosing: education, environment, equality, health, peace, or poverty.[79] Comparing these categories to the sustainable development goals, the overlap is evident.

As girls compete in this challenge, they start by exploring local issues, which relates directly to ISTE Student Standard: Global Collaborator 7D: "Students explore local and global issues and use technologies to work with others to investigate solutions."[80] They are conducting research into the problem of their choosing, which relates directly to ISTE Student Standard: Knowledge Constructor 3A: "Students plan and employ effective research strategies to locate information and other resources for their intellectual or creative pursuits."[81] They must also develop a mobile app that addresses a solution for the problem.

In developing this app, girls are deploying all the ISTE student substandards for the computational thinker strand: "Students develop and employ strategies for understanding and solving problems in ways that leverage the power of technological methods to develop and test solutions":

5A Students formulate problem definitions suited for technology-assisted methods, such as data analysis, abstract models, and algorithmic thinking, in exploring and finding solutions.
5B Students collect data or identify relevant data sets, use digital tools to analyze them, and represent data in various ways to facilitate problem solving and decision making.
5C Students break problems into component parts, extract key information, and develop descriptive models to understand complex systems to facilitate problem solving.
5D Students understand how automation works and use algorithmic thinking to develop a sequence of steps to create and test automated solutions.[82]

Finally, when the girls prepare for the pitch fest, they must figure out how they will market their app to the judges, including information about exactly what problems they are seeking to solve and how the app they've created will allow them to reach a community-wide solution. This is where ISTE Student Standard: Creative Communicator 6D comes in: "Students publish or present content that customizes the message and medium for their intended audience."[83] As the girls develop their app, they must also remember who their audience is. During the pitch fest, they get to hone in on their communication and presentation skills, which serves them well in their future endeavors.

Getting Started

The nice thing about the Technovation Challenge is that girls don't need to have previous experience in coding. Girls simply need to be open to learning and to making a difference in the world. When deciding how to get girls interested in this incredible event, work with the willing and let them influence their friends.

Getting this off the ground in my school took a little bit of work. I started by contacting the high school Geek Girls chapter. They are dedicated to coming together to help others while also learning about how to use and create with technology. From these six girls, there was one who was quite interested in the challenge. I sold her on the idea of participating, as it could be used as her Catalyst project[84].

The Catalyst program is one that students must complete in their junior or senior years. It is now a graduation requirement. The purpose of Catalyst is for students to explore something they are interested in or passionate about and to make something that reflects that interest or passion. More specifically, "A catalyst project is a cultural, instructional, and course-specific student-directed self-study project where students work with a mentor in a relevant field on a school-based to work-based learning experience, aimed at a specific and strategic, measurable, attainable, results-oriented, and time-bound goal."[85] It's an inquiry-based approach to learning where the students explore a personal passion, connecting with experts, having a mentor to guide them on the journey, and sharing their learning at the end of the term. What makes this program unique is that students must create something based on their learning.

The Technovation Challenge integrates with this beautifully, as girls must come together to create an app that solves a problem. In doing this, the girls are learning about the many problems of the world, and they are charged with coming up with a creative solution by way of making an app that would aid in solving the problem of their choosing. Thus, getting the high school girl(s) interested was easy, as they had a dual and clearly defined purpose.

Getting middle and elementary school girls interested was a whole other worthy feat.

Because my titled job had me working in the elementary school, I was on a first-name basis with the girls in grade five. For the Technovation Challenge, girls must be at least ten years of age, which brings the demographic to grades five and up. I started with the girls I knew and approached my Girls Coding Club participants, both current and previous members. From that initial familiarity, I got a list of girls (many of whom were now in middle school) from our Robotics Club that was led by our GATE (Gifted and Talented Education) teacher.

There was never an expectation to have twenty girls involved, so I found no need to establish a formal after-school program. Once the first few girls had signed up, something organic began to happen. They started inviting their friends to join them. I was over the moon with excitement. This is exactly how it was supposed to work out.

With the over-communication of policies within our schools, sometimes we forget the most important piece: the well-being and connectedness of the students we serve.

The thing with the Technovation Challenge is that it is completely participant driven, giving the girls full autonomy on how to create project teams. My job as their mentor is to be just that: an adult who is actively providing information and support as they work together to build creative solutions to the world's problems.

With the global reach of the Technovation Challenge, girls are encouraged to think globally and act locally. What is a world problem, and what does it look like on the scale of their current community? By finding problems, the girls are able to fully embrace the skills outlined in the Future Work Skills 2020 report.[86] The world needs more problem finders. We are not perfect. If we continue assuming that everything is A-OK, then we're only fooling ourselves. When girls seek out the problems in our communities, they're beginning to think like coders who look for the bugs and viruses in programs. By having them create an app that solves a given problem, we're empowering them to combine their coding skills with a purpose that is near and dear to their hearts.

When I met with the high school Geek Girls, one made a connection between her love for protecting the environment and how she might be able to create an app that provides a solution to this global problem. You see, it's all about the purpose. This girl knew her *why*; now with this Technovation Challenge opportunity, she was able to embrace a means to implementing the *how* while also learning a new skill that will benefit her in the future. It's not about doing one thing or another; it's about how we can combine both to have a more profound impact on the footprint we leave in this world.

While introducing this opportunity to an interested group of girls one Friday during a break from their regularly scheduled courses, I found that I was able to easily sell them this idea because it fit with their core values. They literally said they wanted to do something they were passionate about.

Here's how it all started.

Upon meeting with the high school Geek Girls group and sending out some targeted e-mails to girls who might be interested based on their current or previous extracurricular activities, I created an information session to share the details of the Technovation Challenge. From the thirty-two girls I had sent a calendar invite to, only four responded affirmatively. The initial invite had the information session taking place over the course of one hour in a central part of our school, from 11:00 a.m. to 12:00 p.m. I thought this might be a good time until I realized that our grade-five girls wouldn't have a break until 12:40 p.m. I extended the information session from one hour to two. The sessions themselves would be only ten to twenty minutes long, and girls would come whenever was convenient for them to hear about the opportunity.

The first group consisted of two grade-five girls. They were excited about the opportunity to create a working app. Having only used Scratch in their previous coding experience; these girls were ready for the next step up. They would be using MIT App Inventor to develop their apps for the Technovation Challenge.

The second group was more diverse, containing three grade-six students, one grade-ten student, and one grade-eleven student. The grade-six students had been my students for their grade-four and grade-five years, so I knew them pretty well. The two high school students, on the other hand, were completely foreign to me. These two girls were friends, and the grade-eleven girl was taking the Catalyst course in the upcoming spring quarter. I let her know that the Catalyst program director was a friend of mine, and that he had given the Technovation Challenge two thumbs-up for any girls who wanted to participate in the challenge and have it count as their Catalyst projects.

The number-one challenge that students have with a Catalyst project is figuring out what in the world they want to pursue as their self-study project. *Passion* is something that is hard to define. Thus, when students are put in a situation where they have a plethora of choices, all of their own creation, it can be hard to focus on just one. The second biggest challenge is the time-management aspect. Creating something that is "specific, strategic, measurable, attainable, results-oriented, and time-bound" over the course of one semester, while juggling life and the requirements of other courses can be pretty intense. The intensity grows if you don't have a clear vision of what you are trying to achieve.

The Technovation Challenge gives girls the *how*. They must define their *why* by finding a problem in their community or in the greater world that relates to the environment, peace, poverty, education, equality, or health and is aligned with the sustainable development goals. The program gives them the basic stepping-stones for understanding coding and getting to know the basics of how to create a functional app. The girls are the ones who ideate, plan, and present the solutions to the problem of their choosing by creating an app that helps solve the problem in some way and then pitching that app. to a group of international judges.

When the high school girls were in the information session and began putting the pieces together for how they might create an app. that solves an environmental problem, you could feel the energy in the room. It was as though the greatest "aha" moment in the entire universe had occurred because these girls realized they could learn how to create an app. while helping a cause they were passionate about, which also supported the work they were required to complete as part of the Catalyst project.

My heart fluttered as their energy filled the room. Anyone who works with high school students knows that it's hard to excite them. When that moment occurs, one must grab it and hold on to it.

As the high school girls exited the room following the completion of our information session, they weren't more than two feet outside the room when I heard one girl say to the other, "This is so *cool*!"

Passion sparked.

Mission accomplished!

Part 4

Linking Coding into the Curriculum

This section provides a general guide for integrating coding into the curriculum of several content areas.

The best way to expose our girls to coding is to integrate it in a purposeful way with something we're already doing. When you assign students the task of creating a game or a story using some block-based program, circle back around and define the *why*. What is the purpose in creating the story or game? When students know the why, and they are given the freedom to explore their own personalized *how*, they are better able to focus on what they are doing instead of getting distracted by all the bells and whistles that exist within a program.

There's been significant talk about coding lately—from the first Hour of Code event hosted in December 2013 by Code.org to countries like Denmark, England, and Finland incorporating coding into their curriculum. In the United States, several states have adopted computer-science initiatives whereby every student will learn how to code at some point in his or her academic career.

Maybe your school or district fits within this category. Maybe you are a little behind the curve. Maybe you have coaches who come in to teach explicit coding to your kids. Maybe you view it as just one more thing. Regardless of your reasoning, this section will help provide you with meaningful integration opportunities. This section will provide baseline examples that you can take as is or that you can modify and level up in your class.

I do have one ask for the content shared in this section. Let's create a learning community! For every activity that you incorporate or remix from the content shared within this section, write a short explanation and share it on Twitter using *#sdg5code.*

Coding Progressions

Differentiating between Programming and Coding

Throughout this book, you've primarily seen the word *coding* used instead of *computer programming*. In current pop culture, the term is *coding*. Computer programming is the action or process of writing computer programs, providing a computer with coded instructions for the automatic performance of a particular task. *Coding* is a catchier (and more succinct) way of saying computer programming.

Logic versus Syntax

When learning how to code, there are essentially two different types of processes. One is through block-based manipulation, and the other is through scripting. Some newer programs infuse both block-based and script-based coding, allowing the programmer to toggle between the two.

Block-based coding is centered on logic, as you can visually see the pieces you're putting together and the impact the order will have on the characters or pieces within your program. Learning how to code through the use of blocks is beneficial for students as they are able to logically make sense of the order of the pieces within their code. In the vast majority of available programs, the blocks are predetermined, so students need only to grab a block from the bank and place it in their programs.

The starting point for learning coding is block-based coding. College and university professors will often begin an Introduction to Computer Programming course with a series of block-based coding activities to enforce or reinforce the learners' logic on how the pieces of a program work together.

On the other hand, syntax refers to the arrangement of words and phrases to create well-formed programs. When we work with nonvisual scripting languages, such as C++, Javascript, Ruby, and Python, then we are working with syntax. Syntax is the fine details that allow a computer script to function. Think of syntax as a spelling test where a sentence must have words correctly ordered with proper grammar mechanics. If one single punctuation, capitalization, or word placement is wrong in the sentence, then the grade on the spelling test decreases. The same thought can be applied to the writing of literary papers. If the story doesn't have the correct punctuation, capitalization, word choice, or flow, then the reader may have a hard time understanding the content.

In editing student narratives for the insertion into a collaborative, published book, I scanned their writing for basic spacing and punctuation and adjusted fonts and sizes to make the entire piece readable. While conducting a quick review of each student's narrative, I found myself getting highly confused by a few of the narratives. Spacing didn't exist, commas were in the wrong places, and the wrong letters were capitalized. And to think, I wasn't even fully reading the content of their stories. My understanding based on these visual mistakes had discouraged me from reading any further.

Script-based coding works in the exact same way. If one piece is wrong, then the program simply won't work. All it takes is leaving off one semicolon or failing to put proper spacing between pieces of the code to prevent the program from working at all.

Logic, first and foremost, is imperative for students to better understand how the syntax works. Logic is a system or set of principles underlying the arrangement of elements in a computer or electronic device to perform a specified task[87]. Logic is all about knowing what the pieces mean, and how they work. Syntax is about creating the correct pieces and putting them in the correct places to make a program work.

Once, when I had two high school boys helping out with my after-school coding club, they saw block-based coding for the first time as they went around the room helping my elementary-aged students think through their programs. At the conclusion of our club, the high school boys told me they wished their advanced placement computer-science teacher would have started the course with block-based coding instead of diving headfirst into script-based coding.

Foundations are everything. Having a firm understanding of the logic behind a program enables students to understand the syntax that goes into it when they later work with script-based coding.

Integration in Math

In math class, as students begin to learn about angles and geometric shapes, this would be one of the best times for them to learn how to code as well. Using Scratch, students can create a question-asking game that finds the measurement of angles in a triangle. Students can also apply mathematical reasoning to decision-making processes. The possibilities are endless!

Within this math section, we will focus on some easy ways to integrate coding activities into your math curriculum. Although the focus here is on explicit integration with the CCSS, each standard description will be spelled out so that you can find the best point of insertion within your own curriculum.

Mathematical Practices

In the CCSS, the one series of math standards that remains consistent throughout grades K–12 are the mathematical practice standards. These standards are as follows:

MP.1 Make sense of problems and persevere in solving them.
MP.2 Reason abstractly and quantitatively.
MP.3 Construct viable arguments and critique the reasoning of others.
MP.4 Model with mathematics.
MP.5 Use appropriate tools strategically.
MP.6 Attend to precision.
MP.7 Look for and make use of structure.
MP.8 Look for and express regularity in repeated reasoning.[88]

In learning how to code, students must consistently make sense of problems and persevere in solving them (MP.1). When we dive into the coding process, the series of mathematical practice standards applies to *how* we approach the learning acquisition of coding. The other mathematical standards that center on things like number sense, algebraic reasoning, order and operations, and geometry focus more on *what* we are learning. One can stand to reason that through the iterative process of learning how to code, students are consistently using at least MP.1 as they tackle their coding problems.

When students are working on pair programming, there may be times when they disagree with one another. When this occurs, they should construct viable arguments and critique the reasoning of others (MP.3). This is all about utilizing logical points to support one another's learning.

Building a working program pertains to having the right pieces in the right places; thus, students must attend to precision, ensuring the quality, condition, and accuracy of their respective programs is on point (MP.6). Remember, if one piece is wrong, then the whole program is wrong.

In using loops within a program, students must look for and express regularity in repeated reasoning (MP.8). Loops allow a program to run in a simplified fashion. They shave time off from the work that the programmer would have to manually compose. By finding and implementing loops, programmers can make a more succinct program, allowing them to purposefully allocate their time to working out the bugs within a program.

Numbers in Base Ten

The numbers in base ten (NBT) standards in the CCSS exist only for grades two through five. Beginning in grade six, these NBT standards transform into the number system (NS) standards. With NBT standards, it's all about understanding place value. The following is the explicit standard language for NBT.1 across grades two through five:

Table 16.1: CCSS Numbers in Base Ten Standard 1[89]

2.NBT.1	Understand that the three digits of a three-digit number represent amounts of hundreds, tens, and ones; for example, 706 equals 7 hundreds, 0 tens, and 6 ones.
3.NBT.1	Use place value understanding to round whole numbers to the nearest 10 or 100.
4.NBT.1	Recognize that in a multidigit whole number, a digit in one place represents ten times what it represents in the place to its right. For example, recognize that 700 ÷ 70 = 10 by applying concepts of place value and division.

Table 16.1: CCSS Numbers in Base Ten Standard 1, cont'd

5.NBT.1	Recognize that in a multidigit number, a digit in one place represents ten times as much as it represents in the place to its right and one-tenth of what it represents in the place to its left.

Beginning as early as second grade, these NBT standards could be used as students create the movement variables for their characters. At this age level, students are focused on block-based coding activities, many of which integrate the use of variables into the program. (See chapter 9 for more information on vocabulary terms.)

This place-value knowledge can be built on and put to use when it comes to creating an item (or a sprite) that possesses some type of movement. Movement is characterized by some form

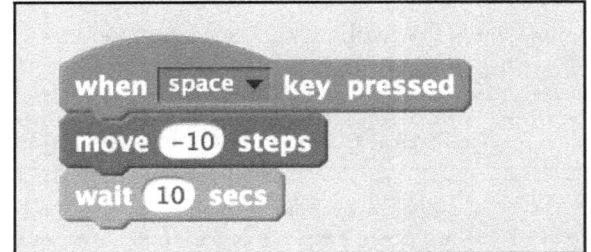

Figure 16.1: Scratch blocks showing whole number wait time

of measurement, whether it be distance or speed. When using a block-based coding application, students can use "wait blocks" or "move blocks" to exemplify how far or for how long their sprite should move. Using a distance block where the sprite moves ten steps is exponentially different from having the character move only one step.

Wait blocks are very similar. In a wait block, the variable within the block

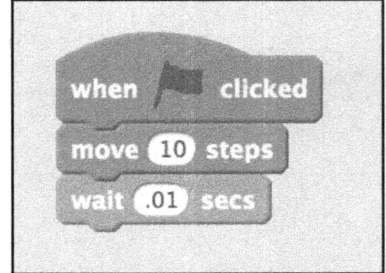

Figure 16.2: Scratch blocks showing decimal wait time

establishes how much time will pass before an action occurs. Having a wait time of ten seconds is very long. When students choose this variable of time, they're able to experience just how long the wait period will last for. Very quickly, students notice how long ten seconds is when compared to one second. Conversely, when students are trying to make an option occur faster, they would need to use a smaller measurement of time. Having students experiment with decimals by choosing a wait time of 0.1, 0.01, or 0.001 helps them to see that the more zeroes that exist to the right of the decimal correlates to the smaller amount of time there is between actions. This understanding links back to NBT in regards to place value, as students are able to visually see how a smaller number generates a shorter timed transition.

Operations and Algebraic Thinking

In the CCSS, 4.OA.5 states that grade-four students will "generate a number or shape pattern that follows a given rule. Identify apparent features of the pattern that were not explicit in the rule itself. For example, given the rule 'Add 3' and the starting number 1 generates terms in the resulting sequence and observes that the terms appear to alternate between odd and even numbers. Explain informally why the numbers will continue to alternate in this way."[90]

When students use loops within their programs, this is exactly what they are doing. Recall from chapter 9 that a loop is a specified piece that repeats the program it contains. Some loops will allow a program to repeat forever. Some will allow the program to repeat for a specific number of times. Some loops will even allow the program to repeat until a specific action occurs.

The great thing about loops is that they can contain any type of pattern. Have students create drawings in programs that repeat a pattern they have created. This can be done with the repeat (a.k.a. loop) block. In doing this, students can demonstrate their understanding of multiplicative procedures and patterns that follow a specific rule.

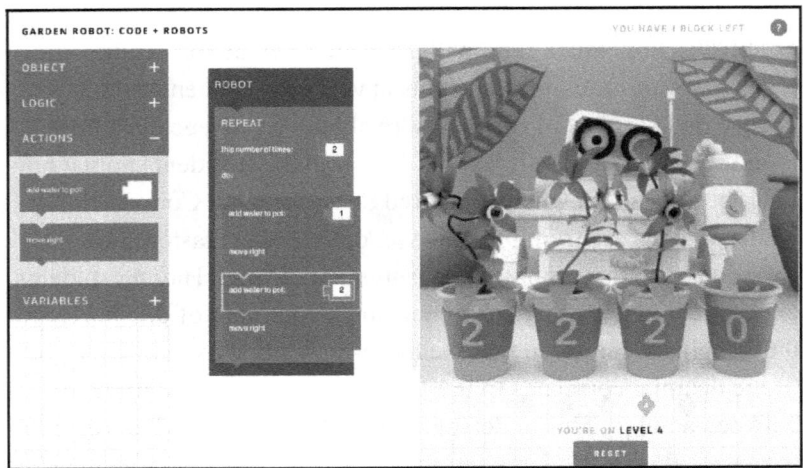

Figure 16.3: Made with Code Garden Robot activity Stage 4

In the preceding garden robot example, students must find the pattern that tells the robot when to water the pot in order to make the flower grow and when to move on to the next pot. In this example, you see that although there is a pattern, there are additional pieces that the programmer must account for. The pattern exists in the program, but it is not the only piece of the program. Thus, when students are looking for patterns within a program, they are thinking like a programmer. They can identify the pattern, see how often it repeats, and then add any additional blocks to the outside of the loop to account for the extra actions that don't exist within the pattern itself.

Measurement and Data

Measurement and data standards provide some of the greatest learning impacts when they are integrated with coding. According to the CCSS, grade-four students have the following two standards that integrate beautifully with coding activities:

Table 16.2: CCSS Measurement and Data Standards[91]

4.MD.5	Recognize angles as geometric shapes that are formed wherever two rays share a common endpoint and understand concepts of angle measurement.
4.MD.6	Measure angles in whole-number degrees using a protractor. Sketch angles of specified measure.

When the movie *Frozen* came out in 2013, was an instant hit. When this happened, Code.org took its characters and turned them into a *Frozen*-themed coding activity. Located at Studio.Code.org, the *Frozen*-themed puzzles are all about having your character skate around to create specific shapes.

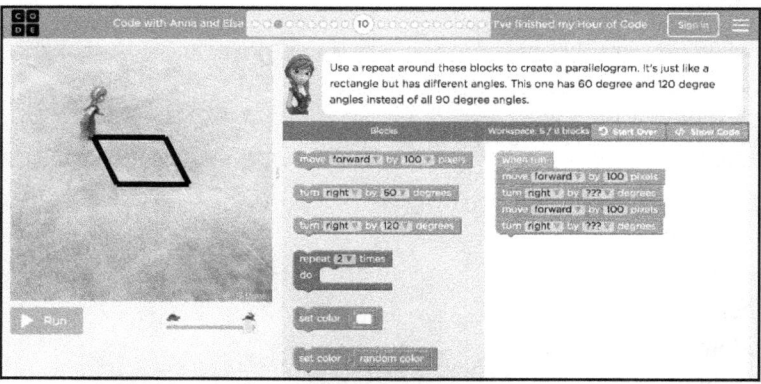

Figure 16.4: Code with Anna and Elsa program, Stage 10

The great thing here is that through this program, students also learn about angle measurements. Within all the Code.org programs (as of the publishing of this book), any program that has the word *artist* in front of it will integrate angles and measurement in some way.

Within these programs, there is a great opportunity to take initiative and teach students about degrees and angles as well as complementary angles and supplementary angles:

- *Angle*: A geometric shape that is formed wherever two rays share a common end point.
- *Degree*: A unit of measurement of angles, 1/360 of the circumference of a circle.
- *Complementary angle*: Either of two angles whose sum is 90 degrees.
- *Supplementary angle*: Either of two angles whose sum is 180 degrees.

When students were completing their programs on Tynker, I had one girl ask for my help in understanding how to make her character flip. I first asked her to clarify what she meant by a flip. She explained that she wanted it to face in the opposite direction. Using the blocks that were available, I asked her which one she thought she might use. She had no idea. She was in third grade, so angles and turns were not related to her academic knowledge. We took the problem to the board. There I drew a circle. I labeled it, telling her that the whole circle has 360 degrees in it and that a degree was a piece of the interior of a circle. I then drew a line through the circle, cutting the circle in half. I asked her how many degrees were in each part of the circle.

Figure 16.5: Drawing a circle to understand degrees

"One hundred eighty degrees," she responded.

Taking this new knowledge, I cut half of the circle in half again and asked her to give me the new degree measurement.

"Ninety degrees," she responded.

As quickly as the answer came out of her mouth, she dived straight into explaining her thinking to me.

"If this angle equals one hundred eighty degrees, and this angle equals ninety degrees, then this angle would equal two hundred seventy degrees," she exclaimed.

Excited by this new realization, she darted back to her seat and began applying her newly acquired knowledge. Putting together the understanding of angles provided her with the opportunity to make the program that she desired. It wasn't about teaching angles just to teach angles. It was about applying the understanding of angles and their measurements to create a program she could be proud of. Remember, purpose and passion go together. Thus, the more opportunities we provide for our students to integrate coding into different subjects, the more likely they are to see how it can be used in new and innovative ways.

With supplementary angles, the important nugget here is understanding that a straight line has a 180-degree angle measurement. Using this knowledge, students can begin to apply this understanding to the creation of shapes.

Take a square, for instance. In creating a program that draws a square, students quickly understand that the square has four equal sides and four equal angles. Thus, in putting together their programs, they would have something like this:

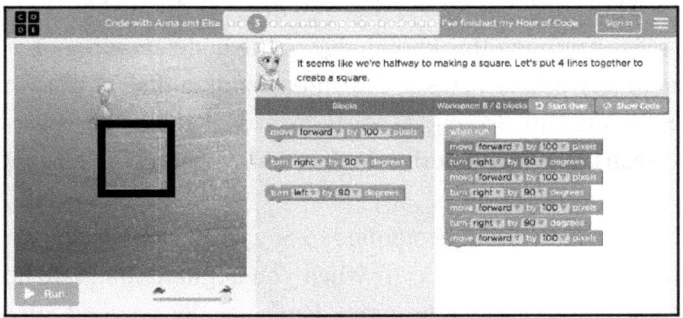

Figure 16.6: Code with Anna and Elsa activity – Stage 3

Using a loop, they could also create their programs to look something like this:

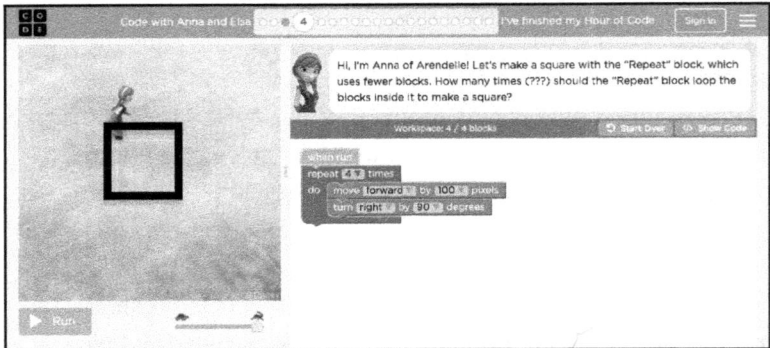

Figure 16.7: Code with Anna and Elsa activity – Stage 4

The challenging part here arises when students begin to discover non-quadrilateral shapes. Take a pentagon, for example. In a pentagon, there are five sides and five interior angles. Thus, our understanding of complementary or supplementary angles would not aid us in this case. To solve this drawing challenge, students would need to find the supplementary angle degree measurement. Because the pentagon has five equal sides and five equal angles, we know that the sum of interior angle measurements equals 360 degrees. Thus, one can reason that 360 degrees divided by 5 equals 72 degrees. Applying this knowledge to the understanding of supplementary angles leads to the understanding that 72 plus some number equals 180. Taking 72 away from 180 gives you 108, which means that each interior angle within a pentagon is equal to 108 degrees.

This math could be applied to any equilateral shape. The place where it gets tricky is when you begin to integrate non-equilateral shapes into the program. Code.org does a great job of building up to this, as their *Frozen* program starts the user off with drawing a line, then an angle, and then a square. By level ten, the user must program Anna to draw a parallelogram.

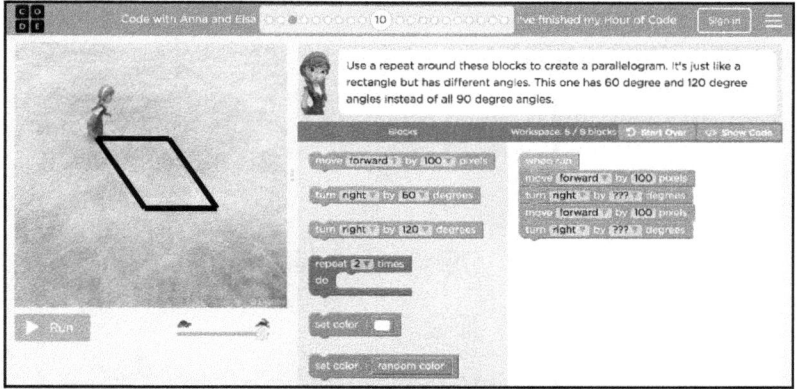

Figure 16.8: Code with Anna and Elsa activity – Stage 10 start

In this activity, the student is given the basic move measurements and must determine the degree of each turn. This is where complementary angles come into play. The shape is a parallelogram, which means that it has equal angle measurement on opposite sides and it has complementary angles on adjacent sides. Within this shape, we can use assumptions. One angle is obtuse, the other angle is acute, and no angle is equal to 90 degrees. Putting this knowledge altogether, $x + y = 180$.

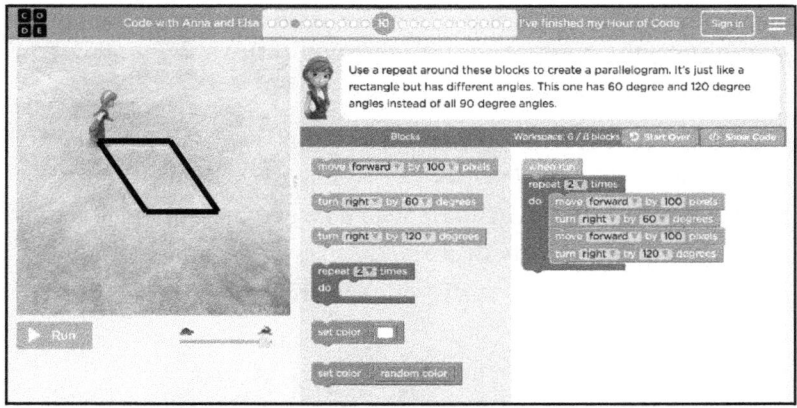

Figure 16.9: Code with Anna and Elsa activity – Stage 10 complete

If x is greater than 90 degrees, then y is less than 90 degrees. Through the use of the drop-down tool, students can quickly reason that angle x equals either 45 or 60 degrees, and angle y equals 120 degrees. Knowing that angle y has only one option, 120 degrees, then the students can stand to reason that angle x is equal to 60 degrees.

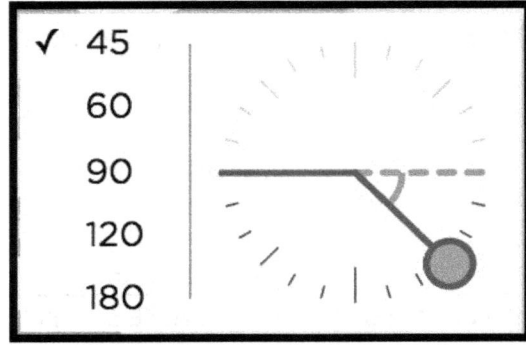

Figure 16.10: Code.org dropdown angle tool

The mere concept of an angle or a degree is often taught as a stationary object on paper. By providing students with the opportunity to code the movement that creates the angle, they are better able to understand how the angle was formed and why it is either an acute, obtuse, or a right angle. Giving these definitions to students as they explore the concept, creation, and manipulation of angles provides them with a vocabulary bank that complements their coding actions and that can be naturally transferred into their mathematical assignments:

- *Acute angle*: An angle with a degree measurement that is less than ninety degrees.
- *Obtuse angle*: An angle with a degree measurement that is more than ninety degrees.
- *Right angle*: An angle with a degree measurement that is ninety degrees.

Integrating these definitions into the appropriate coding activities will give your students endless "aha" moments as they use their background knowledge to deepen understanding of measurement and data concepts. Although this example explicitly highlights a grade-four activity, there does not have to be a defined beginning or end to where such an integration comes into play. Remember the girl I mentioned in the example with the circle activity? She was only in grade three.

Geometry

Geometry tends to be one of those mathematical content areas that students find too abstract. Many will say that if you're a "math person," then you prefer either algebra or geometry, but not both.

In the CCSS, the major geometry standards that easily tie into coding activities exist in grades five, six, and eight:

Table 16.3: Common Core State Standard Geometry Standard[92]

5.G.1	Use a pair of perpendicular number lines, called axes, to define a coordinate system, with the intersection of the lines (the origin) arranged to coincide with the 0 on each line and a given point in the plane located by using an ordered pair of numbers, called its coordinates. Understand that the first number indicates how far to travel from the origin in the direction of one axis, and the second number indicates how far to travel in the direction of the second axis, with the convention that the names of the two axes and the coordinates correspond (e.g., x-axis and x-coordinate, y-axis and y-coordinate).
5.G.2	Represent real-world and mathematical problems by graphing points in the first quadrant of the coordinate plane and interpret coordinate values of points in the context of the situation.
6.G.3	Draw polygons in the coordinate plane given coordinates for the vertices; use coordinates to find the length of a side, joining points with the same first coordinate or the same second coordinate. Apply these techniques in the context of solving real-world and mathematical problems.
8.G.7	Apply the Pythagorean theorem to determine unknown side lengths in right triangles in real-world and mathematical problems in two and three dimensions.

The standards here focus on coordinate planes. One nice thing that many people may be unaware of is that the popular, free program Scratch[93] actually has a coordinate plane. Many of the coding programs that allow you to freely manipulate a character or object around the screen also use a coordinate plane.

In Scratch, when users choose a backdrop, have them choose the "other" category. Choosing this category will allow them to access the XY-grid.

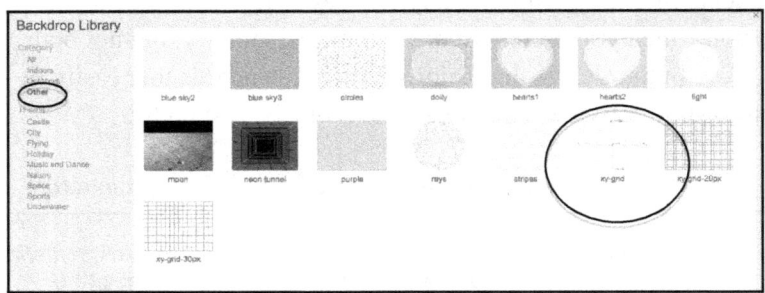

Figure 16.11: Scratch Backdrop Library – "Other" category

With the XY-grid as the backdrop, you could assign such simple activities as having students move their sprite to the third quadrant. To truly level this up, you could have students create a program that draws a specified shape within a specific quadrant. Although it is true that the standard 5.G.2 has students working within the first quadrant only, the reality is that there are four quadrants and that there is not another standard that relates to the other three quadrants.

The important thing to remember is that lack of existence does not imply lack of importance. The first quadrant is highlighted in the standards and is the only one that contains all the positive numbers. But what about the negative numbers?

Leveraging the background knowledge of angle measurements (from grade four), students could create a program that draws a square in the first quadrant and a hexagon in the third quadrant. Here students are empowered to integrate new knowledge with prior knowledge, using coding as a way to demonstrate their understanding of the required content.

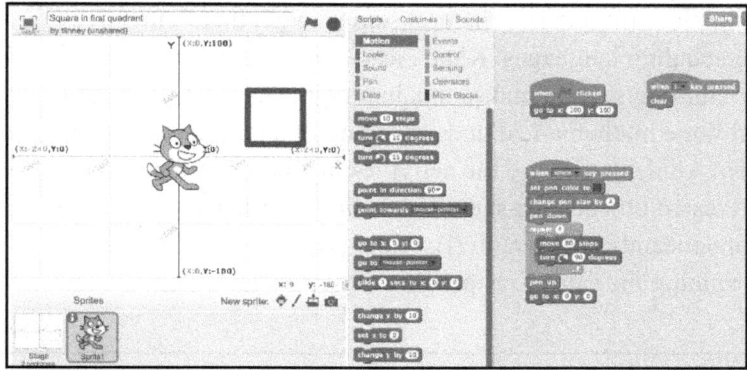

Figure 16.12: Drawing a square in the first quadrant with Scratch

Another great gem of a program is Khan Academy[94]. In August 2012, Khan Academy launched a brand-new addition to their platform: computer science. Khan Academy is not only free but also provides some great videos and forums that allow users to learn new concepts within a community of learners from whom they can receive guidance.

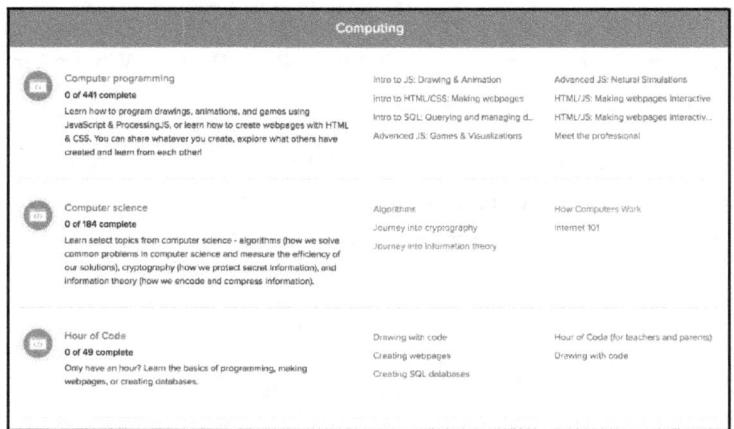

Figure 16.13: Khan Academy's Computing Course options

In several of Khan Academy's computer-science sections, the focus is on Javascript, or HTML. Yes, you read that right, actual script-based coding languages. Once students have developed a solid understanding of Scratch or another block-based coding platform, the next natural step is to get them into understanding languages. Khan Academy's computer programming section makes this jump quite easy. Applying the exact same mathematical understanding of a coordinate plane system, students can use the activities in Khan Academy to design self-created objects in a specific location (x, y). They also integrate the understanding of length (l), width (w), and height (h) in determining the size of shapes that they create.

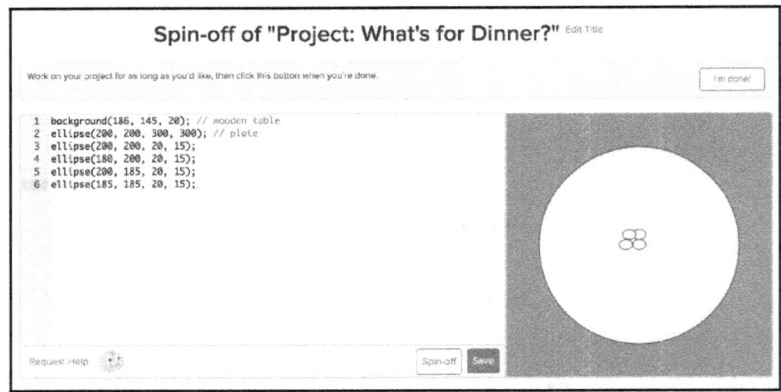

Figure 16.14: Khan Academy's Spin-off of "Project: What's for Dinner?"

Take this example of the "What's for Dinner?" project. Students are given the freedom to create their own plate of food using mathematical concepts as they build and position the shapes for their foods on the plate.

The Number System

Learning about the number system focuses on positive and negative numbers as well as absolute value and rational numbers on a number line. This new topic brings in the basic understanding of coordinate planes that comes from previous coursework in grade five, as students learn how to build on their basic understanding of the coordinate plane system. Within the specific number system standards we'll explore in this section, we will look to leverage the prior knowledge of the first quadrant and level that up with the plotting of points on a graph.

Table 16.4: CCSS – The Number System – Grade 6[95]

6.NS.5	Understand that positive and negative numbers are used together to describe quantities having opposite directions or values (e.g., temperature above/below zero, elevation above/below sea level, credits/debits, positive/negative electric charge); use positive and negative numbers to represent quantities in real-world contexts, explaining the meaning of 0 in each situation.
6.NS.6	Understand a rational number as a point on the number line. Extend number line diagrams and coordinate axes familiar from previous grades to represent points on the line and in the plane with negative number coordinates.
6.NS.7	Understand ordering and absolute value of rational numbers.

Differentiating between positive and negative integers is a concept that students encounter some problems with. By using coding to deepen the understanding of these concepts and applying them to the creation of a program, we're getting students out of the ambiguous environment of a separated understanding and allowing them to apply this new knowledge to their own computer programs.

The most basic way to apply this content knowledge to a computing program starts with using Scratch. Use the XY-grid for your backdrop. From there, create a game that resembles Battleship. In the Battleship game[96], players must guess where the opponent's ship is located without viewing the opponent's board. All the locations for the opponent's fleet are hidden from the other player. The player must then guess a point on the opponent's grid. If the player guesses a point that contains his or her opponent's ship, then the player gets to put a piece on that point. Because the ships can go either latitudinal or longitudinal, the player has to guess all the points that make up the opponent's ship(s).

What's nice about creating a game like this is that students have to understand ordered pairs and figure out which ordered pair could come next in a sequence that would give away the location of the opponent's ship.

Another idea would be to have students build programs where actors (or sprites) move to specific points on a coordinate plane based on an action (a conditional).

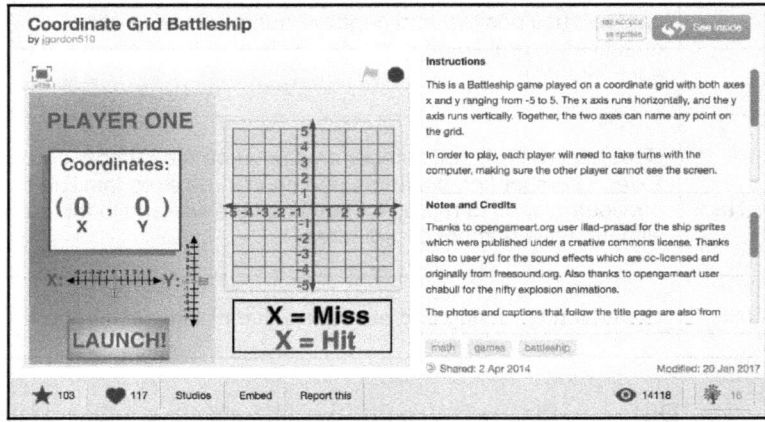

Figure 16.15: Coordinate Grid Battleship game on Scratch

By using coding programs like these to help students apply their understanding of mathematical practices, we're instilling in them an interdisciplinary understanding for how math ties into coding. This generates a self-identified purpose for learning math and coding, as the knowledge of the two together enables the user to create an array of objects and programs that could be incorporated into the creation of digital stories, activities, or games.

Integration in Reading, Writing and Language

This is where the creativity begins to ooze out of our students. When you leverage coding activities within the reading and language arts standards, it brings purpose to reading; it brings reading to life. The best way to understand and digest how coding can be integrated into reading and language arts learning activities is by treating it like learning the mechanics of a language. That's essentially what learning how to code is. It's about learning the various elements that make up a language and communicating those pieces in a way that makes sense to the end user.

Reading Informational Text

Within the reading informational text standards, there exists a plethora of opportunities to integrate reading connections into coding activities. This section will focus specifically on reading informational text, as code is made up of data, and data is information. Highlighting Standard 3 for K–5 on the reading informational text standard, the following is a description of the standards that correspond to each grade level:

Table 17.1: CCSS Reading Informational Text - Standard 3[97]

RI.K.3	With prompting and support, describe the connection between two individuals, events, ideas, or pieces of information in a text.
RI.1.3	Describe the connection between two individuals, events, ideas, or pieces of information in a text.
RI.2.3	Describe the connection between a series of historical events, scientific ideas or concepts, or steps in technical procedures in a text.
RI.3.3	Describe the relationship between a series of historical events, scientific ideas or concepts, or steps in technical procedures in a text, using language that pertains to time, sequence, and cause/effect.
RI.4.3	Explain events, procedures, ideas, or concepts in a historical, scientific, or technical text, including what happened and why, based on specific information in the text.
RI.5.3	Explain the relationships or interactions between two or more individuals, events, ideas, or concepts in a historical, scientific, or technical text based on specific information in the text.

When students work on completing or building programs, their focus is on the process. It's on the *why*, but it's also on the *how*. In making connections between happenings, students are able to understand cause-and-effect relationships. This understanding is best seen through the use of conditionals. Remember the definition for conditionals: a conditional is an "*if this, then that*" statement.

Understanding how conditionals work in their programs allows students to see the impact that actions have. They are able to see what happened and why. This knowledge can transfer from coding to reading, and from reading to coding. This concept of a conditional appears frequently throughout coding programs. Thus, if a student doesn't fully understand it with the first go-round, then he or she will have the chance to understand it again in the future.

As young as kindergarten, students can begin identifying the relationships and connections that exist within their programs. Infusing *how* questions into your inquiry gets students to think about the process, whereas *why* gets them to think about the cause. Do you have an idea as to what you want your students to understand and how it could tie into your standards? Is it all about the process? Is it all about the cause? Or is it a hybrid of the two?

For their explanations of thinking, students could do several things. They could merely speak their thoughts, or they could level it up and write their reasoning down. By communicating their thinking, it's easier to check for understanding when assessing your students' learning.

In addition, this experience in communicating understanding within coding activities can be linked back to the reading curriculum experiences that students encounter when they work within various reading units in their class.

Within standard five of the reading informational text standards for grades two through four, there is an emphasis on structure and text features. In grade two, it begins with the act of knowing and using text features:

Table 17.2: CCSS Reading Informational Text - Standard 5[98]

RI.2.5	Know and use various text features (e.g., captions, bold print, subheadings, glossaries, indexes, electronic menus, icons) to locate key facts or information in a text efficiently.
RI.3.5	Use text features and search tools (e.g., key words, sidebars, hyperlinks) to locate information relevant to a given topic efficiently.
RI.4.5	Describe the overall structure (e.g., chronology, comparison, cause/effect, problem/solution) of events, ideas, concepts, or information in a text or part of a text.

A text feature includes such items as captions, bold print, subheadings, glossaries, indexes, electronic menus, and icons. All these items exist within coding activities. If students get stuck in an area, then they must consult an electronic guide that will help them in their ability to find or create the right solution. In block-based programs, such as Scratch, Tynker, and an array of others, students must navigate through the program, often looking for specifically colored blocks that relate to a given function or action. Understanding how to go about finding and using these features in a coding program allows students to become immersed in the experience of constructively looking for the keys that will enable them to creatively solve the problems within their programs.

Let's look at Scratch. When working with my Girls Coding Club, the girls always ask me questions about how they

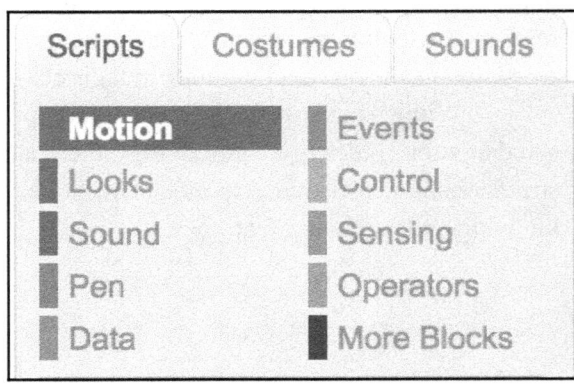

Figure 17.1: Scratch block category menu

can create their programs. Sometimes they just need a wait block or something really simple. However, when it comes to finding where this block is, it is often hard for them to figure out where to find it among the array of block categories to choose from. As the lead learner, I ask them questions:

What does it mean to "wait"?

Which category might we find this block in?

When you ask students questions, instead of giving them answers, it makes them think. Thinking is something that we forget about when we work with students, especially young students. They don't understand things right away, so getting them to think before they demand answers from the lead learner is what we must do if we want them to be active, successful learners rather than just sideliners.

To effectively code, reading is a must. Being able to find and decipher information in a program allows students to take that process and apply it to other curricular areas. With reading, we as educators should be modeling it as a lifelong skill, not as something that is drilled and tested throughout the duration of a student's academic career.

In middle school, the reading informational text standards focus on two areas. One is reading literacy in history/social studies, and the other is reading literacy in science and technical subjects. Within the science and technical subjects category lies a depth of opportunities for the integration of coding:

Table 17.3: CCSS Reading Literacy in Science and Technical Subjects – Standards 3 and 4[99]

RST.6–8.3	Follow precisely a multistep procedure when carrying out experiments, taking measurements, or performing technical tasks.
RST.6–8.4	Determine the meaning of symbols, key terms, and other domain-specific words and phrases as they are used in a specific scientific or technical context relevant to grades six through eight texts and topics.

Middle school is a great time to get students to move from block-based coding to script-based coding. To do this, consider working with learners who have some experience with block-based coding. Remember, block-based coding is about logic. Script-based coding is about syntax. Syntax is the arrangement of words and phrases to create well-formed sentences in a language.

There are a few ways to move into this syntax-based side of coding learning experiences. Although the number of programs that move learners from block to script is limited (as of the publishing of this book), here we will focus on two of these tools and how they work to move students into syntax learning. One is Swift Playgrounds, and the other is Khan Academy.

Swift is the code that Apple uses to create iPhone and iPad apps. In 2016, Apple introduced a free app called Swift Playgrounds. Swift Playgrounds[100] allows learners to easily see what they create in real time, once they hit play. When they do start creating a program, they can either write it out or use the blocks at the bottom of the program that contain the actual Swift code script.

On the left side of their screens, they can read directions for what their characters need to do. Putting it all together is completely up to the students. If they follow each step-by-step guide, then they will be able to successfully create their programs. However, if they leave out a step, then the whole program will not work. This helps students to see why it's important to read.

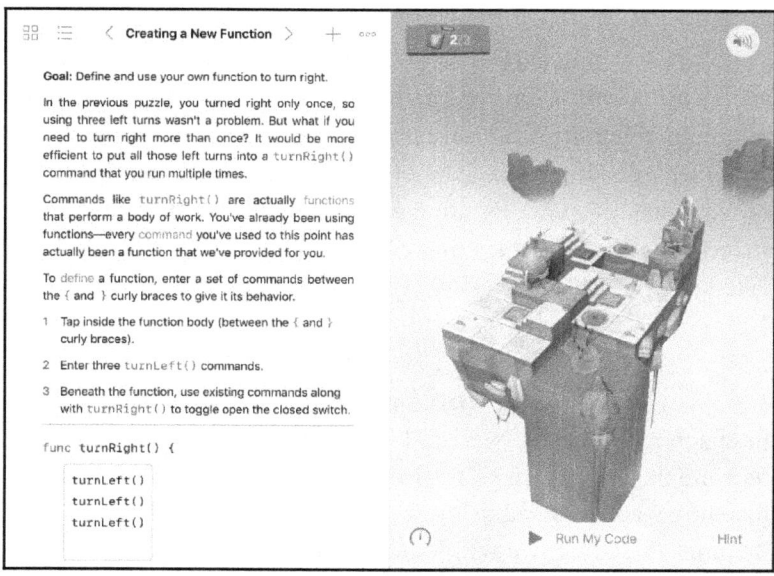

Figure 17.2: Swift Playgrounds – Creating a New Function activity

With Khan Academy (which is also free), students can access its computer programming section. Within this section, they will see some ways in which they can use the reading standards. First, within each learning program, students will see a few types of images.

- The **triangle** is for playing a learning video.

- The **paper** is something to read.

- The **star** is a challenge, and the rocket is a project.

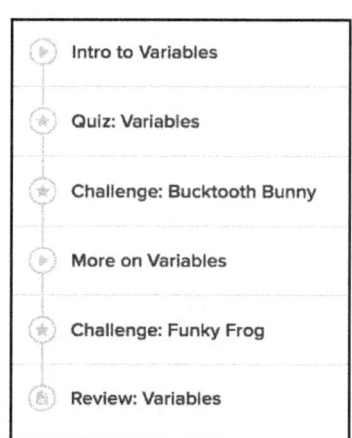

Figure 17.3: Khan Academy program activity icons

Code Equity: Keying Girls Into Coding

The best thing about this is that students who are quickly successful are the ones who go through each step of the learning program. When students get into the challenge or the project, they are given very simple instructions on how to create their programs, or what they must do. Reading these instructions, students can be successful; ignoring them makes the students' learning journey take longer.

Speaking and Listening Standards

In chapter 7, when we were talking about allowing the student to become the expert, we were also talking about the speaking and listening standards and using them in think-pair-share. Here, when it comes to coding, we will focus on the speaking and listening standards in the creation of programs:

Table 17.3: CCSS Speaking and Listening Standard 5[101]

SL.2.5	Create audio recordings of stories or poems; add drawings or other visual displays to stories or recounts of experiences when appropriate to clarify ideas, thoughts, and feelings.
SL.3.5	Create engaging audio recordings of stories or poems that demonstrate fluid reading at an understandable pace; add visual displays when appropriate to emphasize or enhance certain facts or details.
SL.4.5	Add audio recordings and visual displays to presentations when appropriate to enhance the development of main ideas or themes.
SL.5.5	Include multimedia components (e.g., graphics, sound) and visual displays in presentations when appropriate to enhance the development of main ideas or themes.

When students create, they learn. In programs like Scratch, students can create a story that is quite visual, with transitioning backdrops and characters that move and speak. Some coding programs even allow students to draw their own characters and backdrops.

Using a program like this, students can create backdrops and program them to change between specific events. It's like telling a story that takes place between different times and/or places. Students can also create audio recordings in which a sprite speaks when a specific event happens. Maybe the event is based on the movement of another sprite, or maybe it is based on the changing of the background. Either way, students can easily use the blocks to allow sprites to speak at different times.

As students grow stronger in coding, they can create tutorials to teach fellow learners how to create their own programs. It's almost like the videos about *Minecraft*, except that with coding, students focus on teaching one another how to create coding programs.

Writing Standards

The CCSS writing standards change a bit dramatically between grades K–5 to grades six through eight. In K–5, they focus on writing text to examine a topic and convey ideas and information clearly. In grades six through eight, the standard focuses on this, as well as including the narration of historical events, scientific procedures/experiments, or technical processes.

Table 17.4: CCSS Writing Standard 2[102]

W.K.2	Use a combination of drawing, dictating, and writing to compose informative/explanatory texts in which they name what they are writing about and supply some information about the topic.
W.1.2	Write informative/explanatory texts in which they name a topic, supply some facts about the topic, and provide some sense of closure.

Table 17.4: CCSS Writing Standard 2, cont'd

W.2.2	Write informative/explanatory texts in which they introduce a topic, use facts and definitions to develop points, and provide a concluding statement or section.
W.3.2	Write informative/explanatory texts to examine a topic and convey ideas and information clearly.
W.4.2	Write informative/explanatory texts to examine a topic and convey ideas and information clearly.
W.5.2	Write informative/explanatory texts to examine a topic and convey ideas and information clearly.
WHST.6–8.2	Write informative/explanatory texts, including the narration of historical events, scientific procedures/experiments, or technical processes.

Regardless of age, writing is one of those things that students either love or hate.

Here's a short example.

To help challenge a few students in a grade-four teacher's class, I had them begin to learn block-based coding. It started off with two students. To begin, I had the students go through all the lessons in a Code.org program, all twenty of them. Once they got through the program, which was also related to what they were learning in math, I allowed them to build a game. A couple of weeks after working with the two students, the teacher gave me one more. His name was Nigel. Nigel was way ahead of the class as a whole but was now behind in the work that we were doing in this small group. I had him start on the twenty-lesson program, but he couldn't complete it in the twenty minutes we had together.

I remember him asking, "What will I do tomorrow?"

"You'll continue where you left off," I said.

"What if I work on the coding lessons at home? If I finish, then can I start building my game tomorrow?" he begged.

"Sure," I said. "But you'll have to bring me proof that you completed all twenty lessons, minus the ones you got through today."

I expected him to bring me a certificate of completion, which anyone can acquire through a simple Google search, but he didn't. Instead, he brought me a piece of paper with all the solutions to every single lesson handwritten.

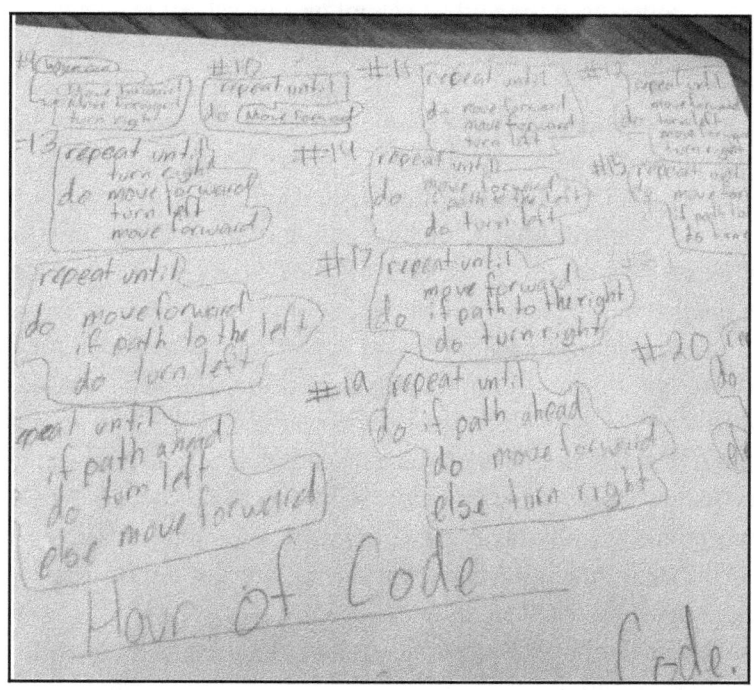

Figure 17.6: Nigel's written version of the instructions for completing an Hour of Code activity from Code.org

I did not tell him to write the solutions. All I told him was that he had to bring me proof that he completed all twenty lessons. Students these days often look for shortcuts to completion, the easy way out. Not Nigel. Nigel had in his mind that in order to prove that he had finished the coding lessons, he would actually have to *complete* them.

This example just goes to show that students will write whatever they put their minds to, especially if it means being allowed to move on to the next level, program, or activity.

Imagine what you could challenge students to write about as they create or complete their coding programs. They could write a guidebook that demonstrates the step-by-step procedures for causing an action to occur.

Students at the middle school or high school level could even advance their integrated learning by writing a comparative analysis of two different coding platforms or languages. This could be done for programs that make the shift from block-based coding to script-based coding. Having students write about this logical shift gets them to understand it in more depth.

Just as reading is fundamental, writing is a way in which we express ourselves. A quote by Justine Musk says, "Reading is the inhale. Writing is the exhale."

Providing students with the opportunity to exhale, through writing, gives them the opportunity to become effective knowledge constructors. The ISTE Student Standard: Knowledge Constructor highlights the importance of and expectation for students to curate a collection of artifacts that demonstrates meaningful learning connections. Combining this curation with a writing-infused goal leads students to construct written knowledge that can be used to help support other students.

Earlier in the book, we discussed the need for purpose to exist within learning opportunities for girls. This opportunity to write a guidebook fulfills that need for purpose while also getting students to write about their specific coding process, circling right back around to their technical writing goals.

Integration in World Languages

In order to be future ready, students should learn how to code. However, being future ready is not only about the ability to do reading, writing, arithmetic, and coding. It's also about understanding how to read and speak in different languages. As schools begin to push coding in classrooms, world language is often the ugly stepchild who is left out or removed. Often we'll see schools declaring that it's either world language or coding, but it can't be both. This chapter will demonstrate how it can be both by showing you examples of how learning a world language while learning coding is highly effective for students.

Just as Spanish, Chinese, Japanese, French, and Italian are languages, coding is also a language.

Think about it.

Languages involve logic for putting the words in the correct order to make a sentence, and they also involve syntax, as spelling, accents, and punctuation can convey specific meanings based on how they are used. Thus, one can reason that coding and world language learning are two peas in the same pod.

Figure 17.7: Code.org language changer location

In Code.org, when you launch one of their company-created programs, look at the bottom-left corner of the screen. You'll see that there's a drop-down menu that will allow you to change the language. Once you change the language, all the blocks and instructions in the program will change as well. This requires students to think on a couple of different levels. Level one is all about decoding the words on the blocks and in the instructions. Level two deals with putting the proper blocks together to make the program run successfully.

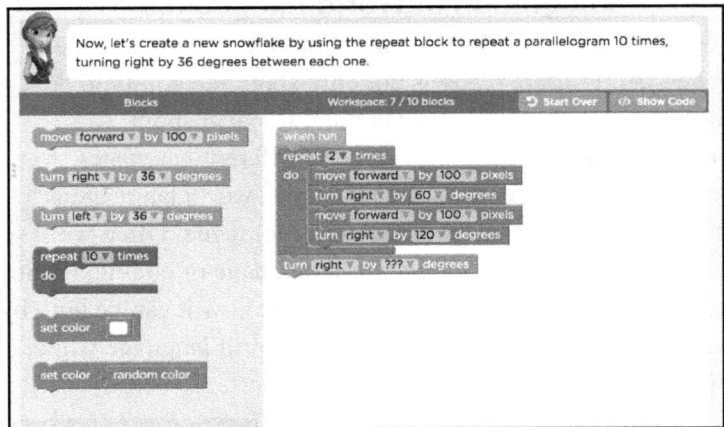

Figure 17.8: Code.org activity in English

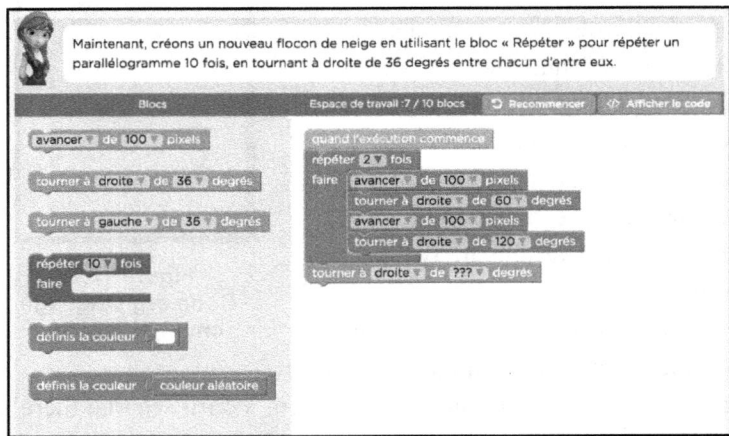

Figure 17.9: Code.org activity in French

Coding in world languages is not about learning in silos. It's about integrating the two content areas to create a more profound learning opportunity. When students are learning a world language and coding together, they are able to amplify their language skills and their critical thinking/problem-solving skills to create a solution.

Coding Resources

There are a variety of tools that one can use to introduce coding to students. All the tools showcased in this section provide you with overviews of programs that have previously been mentioned in this book.

Code.org
Code.org is a free website that gives you the option to create an account to track progress or to use the programs without an account. Their activities span grades K–12, with options for free courses that students can participate in. Established in 2013, the nonprofit Code.org continues to build out its website, providing

learners with block-based as well as script-based coding options. Their website also hosts an array of cartoon-themed activities for learners to engage in as they learn how to code. Some examples of these cartoons include *Angry Birds*, *Frozen*, *Minecraft*, and *Star Wars*.

Figure 18.1: Code.org activities

With Code.org learners can also learn from courses that relate to their specific age-level.

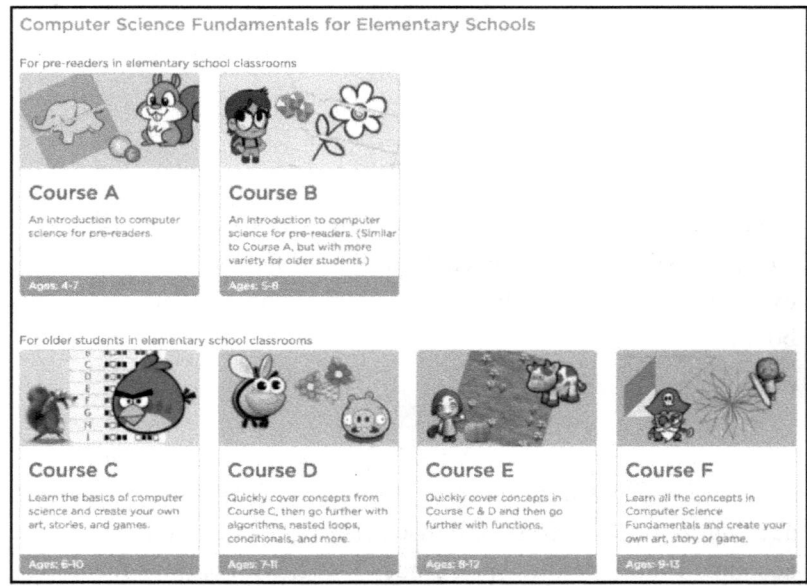

Figure 18.2: Code.org courses for Elementary Schools

One great new innovation that Code.org is making involves the translation of all of its computer science fundamentals courses into 25 different languages. Their curriculum is aligned with the ISTE Standards, and helps to bridge the gap between block-based and script-based coding.

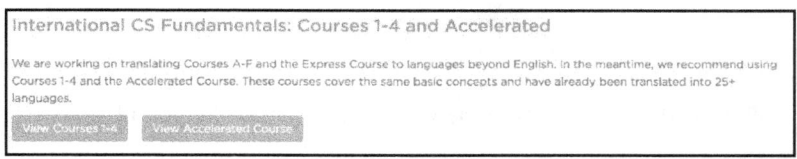

Figure 18.3: Code.org International CS Fundamentals

Khan Academy

Khanacademy.org is a free website that allows users to create accounts to track their learning progress. In the Subjects area of Khan Academy, there exists a Computing section. Within this section, learners have the option to take the following learning

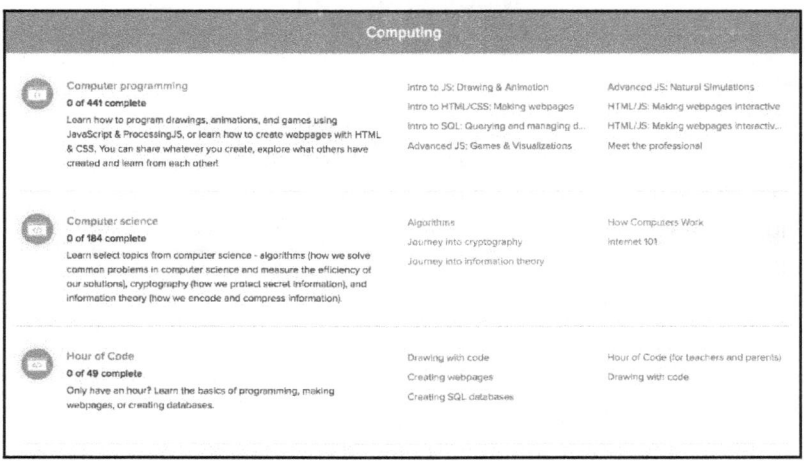

Figure 18.4: Khan Academy Computing course options

paths: computer programming, computer science, Hour of Code, or computer animation.

Each path offers introductory and advanced courses.

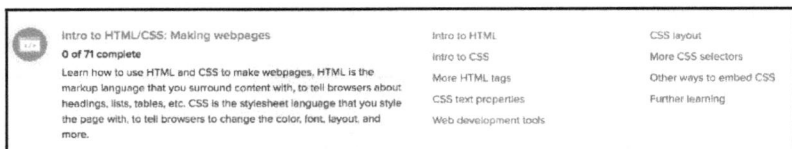

Figure 18.5: Khan Academy Computing course lesson objectives

As students advance through the course, they can watch built-in videos to support their learning. Each course also offers challenges for learners to complete in order to demonstrate what they've learned. Each section ends with a culminating project where the learner will have to combine their new knowledge from that course to create a final project.

Made with Code

Madewithcode.com was established by Google in 2014 as a way to get more girls interested in coding. The site is free, offering a host of block-based projects, mentors, and resources for girls. The projects are activities for the girls to use to practice coding. They integrate a variety of interests—such

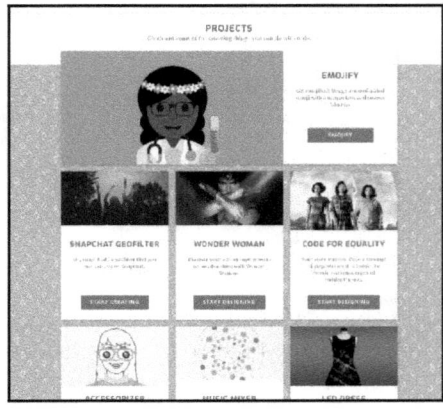

Figure 18.6: Made with Code projects page

as music, art, dance, and fashion—with coding.

The Mentors page provides an array of short videos that highlight women in a variety of tech-infused careers who have made an impact on the world through their work in coding. These videos provide inspiration for our young girls through real-life examples of what other females are doing with code to make a lasting impact.

Figure 18.7: Made with Code mentors page

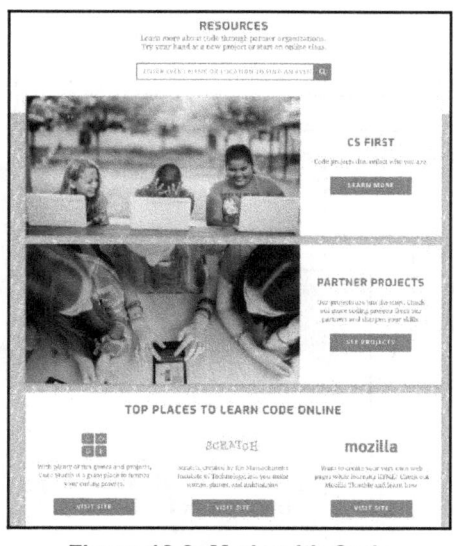

Figure 18.8: Made with Code Resources page

The Resources page offers additional sites for girls who are ready to leap into more advanced coding. Many of the resources on this page provide girls with the opportunity to learn script-based coding in a creative way.

Scratch

Scratch.mit.edu is a block-based program that was launched in 2007 as a downloadable desktop application. The Scratch program that we see today can be accessed through a web browser.

Scratch allows users to remix or create their own projects from scratch. *Get it?*

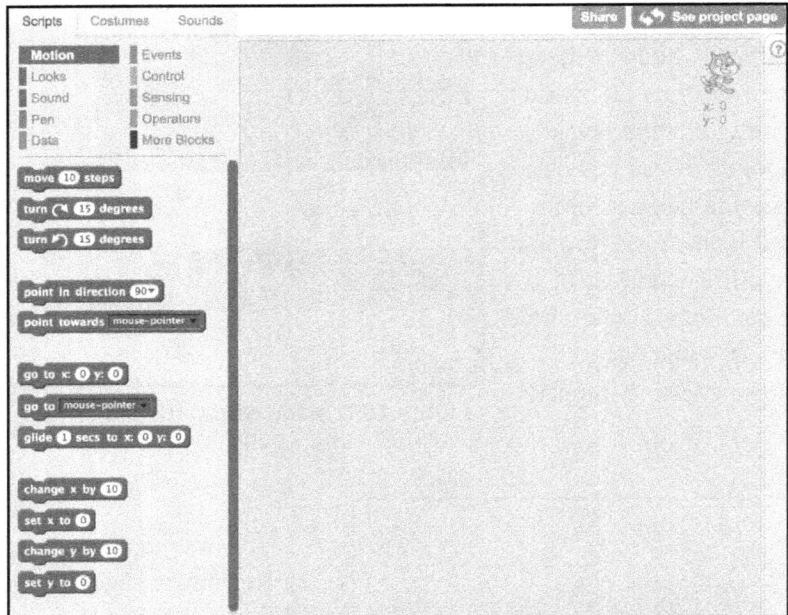

Figure 18.9: Scratch blank coding canvas

Using Scratch, learners can set up free accounts to save their work. They can create as many projects as they want, using a backpack tool to transfer pieces of code from one project to another. Creations can be published to a public community or shared with others via a unique link.

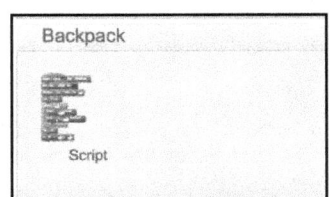

Figure 18.10: Scratch backpack tool

Swift Playgrounds

Swift Playgrounds is an iPad app that works with iOS 10 and above. The app is free and was launched by Apple in 2016 as a way to teach users how to code using Apple's Swift coding language.

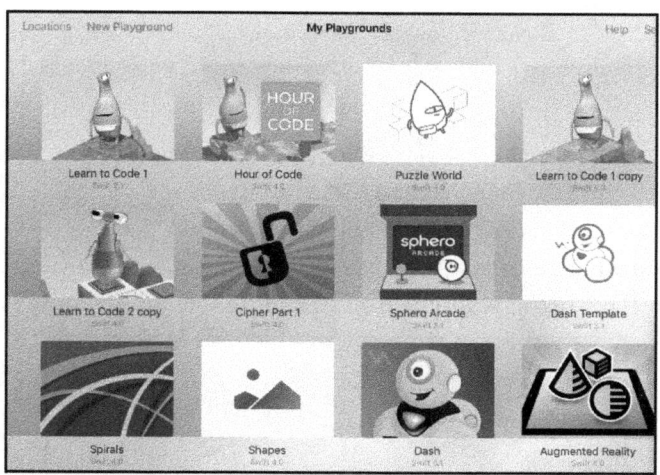

Figure 18.11: Swift Playgrounds playground activities

The app allows users to complete lessons or create their own program altogether, harnessing both the critical thinking and creativity functions of coding. Using Swift Playgrounds, users can see the

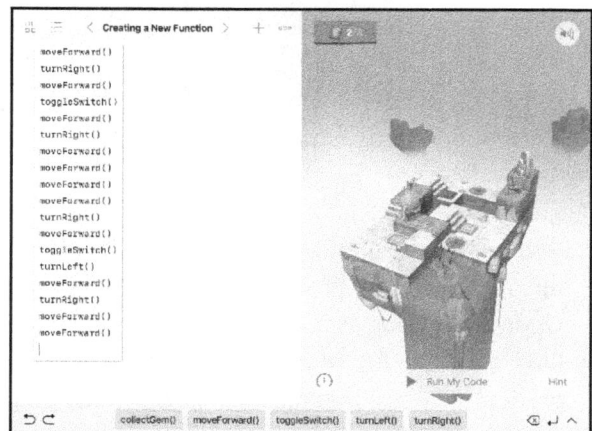

Figure 18.12: Swift Playgrounds "Creating a New Function" activity

Swift coding language in blocks, which aids in easily moving from block-based to script-based coding.

In addition, users can view the actions of their code through an animation that plays to the right side of their code. In this way, users can see the synchronous impact that their codes have on the overall programs.

Technovation Challenge

In chapter 14, we provided an overview of the impact that the Technovation Challenge has on girls and their interests in learning how to code. The Technovation Challenge is completely free and is open to girls ages ten to eighteen years old. The program offers a twelve-week curriculum that walks girls through the creation of an app using MIT App Inventor as well as the marketing and business promotion of the app.

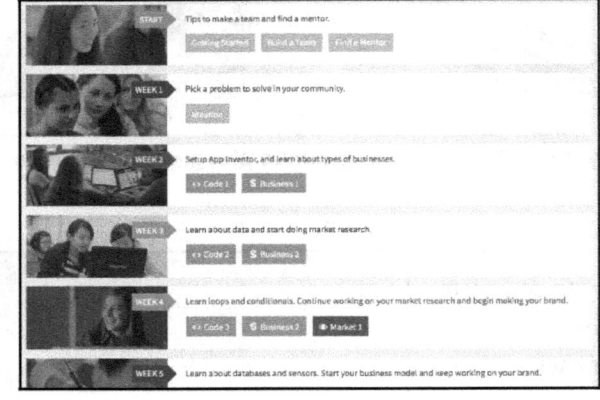

Figure 18.13: Technovation Curriculum page

Upon registering as a mentor or a team member on the site, users have access to the twelve-week curriculum. Though there is no particular device that must be used for this program, MIT App Inventor works only on Android devices.

As we know, getting girls interested in coding is all about linking purpose with passion. The Technovation Challenge offers girls the opportunity to learn how to code through the creation of an app that has some meaningful impact on their communities. This in turn helps create a stronger culture in our society that is centered on gender equity in coding.

Acknowledgements

Special thank you to Ilene Winokur and my wonderful Kickstarter backers for helping to bring this book to life. I'd also like to thank Marc Seigel and Rafranz Davis for allowing me to showcase their teaching practices for other educators to glean from.

Bibliography

[1] John Fuegi and Jo Francis, "Lovelace & Babbage and the Creation of the 1843 'notes,'" *IEEE Annals of the History of Computing* 25, no. 4 (2003): 16–26.

[2] "ENIAC Programmers Project," First Byte Productions, http://eniacprogrammers.org/.

[3] Melfi, Theodore, director. *Hidden Figures*. Twentieth Century Fox Home Entertainment, 2017.

[4] "Most Popular Video Games Released 1984-01-01 to 1984-12-31." *IMDb*, IMDb.com, www.imdb.com/search/title?sort=moviemeter&title_type=game&year=1984%2C1984.

[5] "1984 DOMESTIC GROSSES." *Box Office Mojo*, www.boxofficemojo.com/yearly/chart/?yr=1984.

[6] "'Hard' Sciences: A 'Boy Thing?"." *PBS*, Public Broadcasting Service, 26 Apr. 2012, www.pbs.org/newshour/show/hard-sciences-a-boy-thing.

[7] Henn, Steve. "When Women Stopped Coding." *NPR*, NPR, 21 Oct. 2014, www.npr.org/sections/money/2014/10/21/357629765/when-women-stopped-coding.

[8] Liukas, Linda. *Hello Ruby: Adventures in Coding*. Puffin Books, 2016.

[9] Favilli, Elena, and Francesca Cavallo. *Good Night Stories for Rebel Girls: 100 Tales of Extraordinary Women*. Timbuktu Labs, Inc., 2016.

[10] Marenco, Susan, et al. *Barbie: I Can Be an Actress. I Can Be a Computer Engineer*. Random House Childrens Books, 2013.

[11] Kat, et al. "Kat." *Pamela Ribon*, 17 Nov. 2014, bit.ly/1u2EVjz.

[12] "Tynker | Coding for Kids." *Tynker.com*, www.tynker.com/about/press/2017/12-tynker-joins-forces-with-barbie-on-hour-of-code-programming-experience-to-inspire-girls-to-explore-coding.

[13] "Home." *Technovation*, technovationchallenge.org/.

[14] Conger, Kate. "Exclusive: Here's The Full 10-Page Anti-

Diversity Screed Circulating Internally at Google." *Gizmodo*, Gizmodo.com, 5 Aug. 2017, gizmodo.com/exclusive-heres-the-full-10-page-anti-diversity-screed-1797564320.

[15] Advertising Standards Authority | Committees of Advertising Practice. "ASA Gender Research." *ASA Gender Research - ASA | CAP*, www.asa.org.uk/genderresearch.html.

[16] Magra, Iliana. "Britain Cracking Down on Gender Stereotypes in Ads." *The New York Times*, The New York Times, 18 July 2017, www.nytimes.com/2017/07/18/world/europe/britain-ads-gender-stereotypes.html.

[17] "Gender Gap | Definition of Gender Gap in US English by Oxford Dictionaries." Oxford Dictionaries | English, Oxford Dictionaries, en.oxforddictionaries.com/definition/us/gender_gap.

[18] "Gender Gap." *Gender Gap: The Concise Encyclopedia of Economics | Library of Economics and Liberty*, www.econlib.org/library/Enc/GenderGap.html.

[19] Bureau, US Census. "Library." *1940 Census of Population: Comparative Occupation Statistics 1870-1940*, 1 Jan. 1970, www.census.gov/library/publications/1943/dec/population-occupation.html.

[20] Ibid.

[21] Brown, Anna, and Eileen Patten. "The Narrowing, but Persistent, Gender Gap in Pay." *Pew Research Center*, 3 Apr. 2017, www.pewresearch.org/fact-tank/2017/04/03/gender-pay-gap-facts/.

[22] Galvin, Gabby. "Study: Middle School Is Key to Girls' Coding Interest." *US News*, 20 Oct. 2016, www.usnews.com/news/data-mine/articles/2016-10-20/study-computer-science-gender-gap-widens-despite-increase-in-jobs.

[23] Taves, Max. "Biggest Pay Gap in America: Computer Programmers." *CNET*, CNET, 23 Mar. 2016, www.cnet.com/news/biggest-pay-gap-in-america-computer-programmers/.

[24] "What's Wrong with This Picture?" *Code.org*, code.org/promote.
[25] "AP Program Participation and Performance Data 2017 – Research – The College Board."*Research*, research.collegeboard.org/programs/ap/data/participation/ap-2017.
[26] "Gender Equality and Women's Empowerment." *United Nations*, United Nations, www.un.org/sustainabledevelopment/gender-equality/page/2/.
[27] "Gender Equality and Women's Empowerment." *United Nations*, United Nations, www.un.org/sustainabledevelopment/gender-equality/.
[28] "Gender Equality: Why It Matters." UN.org, Aug. 2016.
[29] Ibid. (28)
[30] *Women at Work: Trends 2016*. International Labour Office, 2016.
[31] Dahan, Mariana. "SDGs Made with Code: Giving Women and Girls the Power to Change the World." *Information and Communications for Development*, 30 Sept. 2016, blogs.worldbank.org/ic4d/sdgs-made-code-giving-young-women-power-change-world.
[32] "Mansplaining." *Merriam-Webster*, Merriam-Webster, www.merriam-webster.com/words-at-play/mansplaining-definition-history.
[33] Uis. *Education : Percentage of Female Teachers by Teaching Level of Education*, data.uis.unesco.org/index.aspx?queryid=178.
[34] Master, Allison, et al. "Programming Experience Promotes Higher STEM Motivation among First-Grade Girls." Journal of Experimental Child Psychology, vol. 160, 2017, pp. 92–106., doi:10.1016/j.jecp.2017.03.013.
[35] Perry, Tekla S. "Want Girls Attracted to Tech? Put an 'A' for 'Art' in STEM." IEEE Spectrum: Technology, Engineering, and Science News, IEEE Spectrum, 14 Dec. 2016, spectrum.ieee.org/view-from-the-valley/at-

work/education/want-girls-attracted-to-tech-put-a-for-art-in-stem.

[36] Beilock, S. L., et al. "Female Teachers' Math Anxiety Affects Girls' Math Achievement." *Proceedings of the National Academy of Sciences*, vol. 107, no. 5, 2010, pp. 1860–1863., doi:10.1073/pnas.0910967107.

[37] Else-Quest, Nicole M., et al. "Cross-National Patterns of Gender Differences in Mathematics: A Meta-Analysis." *Psychological Bulletin*, vol. 136, no. 1, 2010, pp. 103–127., doi:10.1037/a0018053.

[38] *Ally McBeal* is a US-based TV sitcom from the 1990s.

[39] "Inside Out (2015)." *IMDb*, IMDb.com, www.imdb.com/title/tt2096673/.

[40] "Iteration." *Merriam-Webster*, Merriam-Webster, www.merriam-webster.com/dictionary/iteration.

[41] "Family Matters (TV Series 1989–1998)." *IMDb*, IMDb.com, www.imdb.com/title/tt0096579/.

[42] "ISTE Standards for STUDENTS." *ISTE | Standards For Students*, www.iste.org/standards/for-students.

[43] Garun, Natt. "If You Thought Google Glass Is Dorky, Check out What Early Prototypes Looked Like." *Digital Trends*, 20 June 2017, www.digitaltrends.com/computing/early-google-glass-prototypes.

[44] *Saved By The Bell* was a popular US TV show from the 1980s and 1990s.

[45] Ibid.

[46] Ibid.

[47] "Future Work Skills 2020." Institute for the Future for the University of Phoenix Research Institute.

[48] "ISTE Standards FOR EDUCATORS." *ISTE | Standards For Educators*, www.iste.org/standards/for-educators.

[49] "Gender Equality and Women's Empowerment." *United Nations*, United Nations, www.un.org/sustainabledevelopment/gender-equality/.

[50] "The Power of 10: Ten Astonishing Facts about 10-Year-Old Girls." *United Nations Population Fund*, 20 Oct. 2016,

www.unfpa.org/news/power-10-ten-astonishing-facts-about-10-year-old-girls.

[51] "An Educator's Guide to the 'Four Cs.'" *NEA*, www.nea.org/tools/52217.htm.

[52] Ibid.

[53] Wing, Jeannette M. "Computational Thinking Benefits Society." *Social Issues in Computing*, 10 Jan. 2014, socialissues.cs.toronto.edu/index.html%3Fp=279.html.

[54] Ibid.

[55] Magra, Iliana. "Britain Cracking Down on Gender Stereotypes in Ads." *The New York Times*, The New York Times, 18 July 2017, www.nytimes.com/2017/07/18/world/europe/britain-ads-gender-stereotypes.html.

[56] *Gardner's Multiple Intelligences*, www.tecweb.org/styles/gardner.html.

[57] "Third Grade Speaking and Listening Standards." *Common Core Standards*, www.corecommonstandards.com/third-grade-standards/english-language-arts-standards/third-grade-speaking-and-listening-standards/.

[58] "Explain Everything™ on the App Store." *App Store*, 1 Feb. 2016, itunes.apple.com/us/app/explain-everything/id1020339980?mt=8.

[59] "English Language Arts Standards." *English Language Arts Standards | Common Core State Standards Initiative*, www.corestandards.org/ELA-Literacy/.

[60] Azar, Beth. "Math + Culture = Gender Gap?" *Monitor on Psychology*, vol. 41, no. 7, doi:10.1037/e553242010-013.

[61] "Culture." *Merriam-Webster*, Merriam-Webster, www.merriam-webster.com/dictionary/culture.

[62] Try points are given for each unique try at solving a problem, regardless of whether the try was successful.

[63] Fly points are given for every successful attempt.

[64] Murdoch, Kath, and Guy Claxton. *The Power of Inquiry*. Seastar Education, 2015.

[65] Ibid.

[66] Ibid.

67 Ibid.
68 Ibid.
69 Seigel, M. (2018, January 25). Email.
70 Davis, R. (2018, February 21). Email.
71 Ibid.
72 Ibid.
73 Ibid.
74 "Made with Code | Google." *Made w/ Code*, www.madewithcode.com/.
75 Jacobson, Murrey. "Google Finally Discloses Its Diversity Record, and It's Not Good." PBS, Public Broadcasting Service, 28 May 2014, www.pbs.org/newshour/updates/google-discloses-workforce-diversity-data-good.
76 Crook, Jordan. "Google Invests $50 Million In 'Made With Code' Program To Get Girls Excited About CS." *TechCrunch*, TechCrunch, 22 June 2014, techcrunch.com/2014/06/22/google-invests-50-million-in-made-with-code-program-to-get-girls-excited-about-cs/.
77 "Foster Announces State Of The Union Guest." *Congressman Bill Foster*, 16 Jan. 2015, foster.house.gov/media-center/press-releases/foster-announces-state-of-the-union-guest.
78 "Technovation." *Technovation*, technovationchallenge.org/.
79 Ibid.
80 Ibid.
81 Ibid.
82 Ibid.
83 Ibid.
84 "Catalyst Project." *Singapore American School*, www.sas.edu.sg/academics/high/catalyst.
85 Ibid.
86 Ibid.
87 "Logic." *Merriam-Webster*, Merriam-Webster, www.merriam-webster.com/dictionary/logic.
88 "Mathematics Standards." *Mathematics Standards | Common Core State Standards Initiative*,

www.corestandards.org/Math/.

[89] Ibid.

[90] Ibid.

[91] Ibid.

[92] Ibid.

[93] Ibid.

[94] "Computing." *Khan Academy*, www.khanacademy.org/computing.

[95] Ibid.

[96] "Scratch - Coordinate Grid Battleship." *Scratch - Imagine, Program, Share*, scratch.mit.edu/projects/20047731/.

[97] Ibid.

[98] Ibid.

[99] Ibid.

[100] "Swift Playgrounds." *Apple (Singapore)*, www.apple.com/sg/swift/playgrounds/.

[101] Ibid.

[102] Ibid.

About the Author

Tara Linney is an international educator, currently working as an Educational Technology Coach in Singapore. She graduated from the University of South Florida in 2006 with a bachelor's degree in mass communications. After working in the nonprofit and marketing sectors for a few years, Linney decided to go back to school to earn a Master's of Science in the Science of Instruction from Drexel University. She has worked in public and private schools as an EdTech Coach in Washington, DC, Illinois, North Carolina and Singapore. Linney is also an internationally-known speaker on several educational topics including global collaboration, virtual reality, coding in the curriculum, and girls can code.

www.ingramcontent.com/pod-product-compliance
Lightning Source LLC
Chambersburg PA
CBHW070537090426
42735CB00013B/3003